WeightWatchers®

Simple, tasty fish and seafood recipes

Easy Fish

First published in Great Britain by Simon & Schuster UK Ltd, 2013
A CBS Company

Simon & Schuster Illustrated Books, Simon & Schuster UK Ltd,
First Floor, 222 Gray's Inn Road, London WC1X 8HB

www.simonandschuster.co.uk

Simon & Schuster Australia, Sydney
Simon & Schuster India, New Delhi

Weight Watchers Publications: Jane Griffiths, Linda Palmer and Nina McKerlie.

Recipes written by: Sue Ashworth, Sue Beveridge, Tamsin Burnett-Hall,
Cas Clarke, Siân Davies, Roz Denny, Nicola Graimes, Becky Johnson,
Kim Morphew, Joy Skipper, Penny Stephens and Wendy Veale as well
as Weight Watchers Leaders and Members.

Photography by: Iain Bagwell, Steve Baxter, Steve Lee, Juliet Piddington
and William Shaw.
Project editor: Nicki Lampon.
Design and typesetting: Martin Lampon.

Colour reproduction by Dot Gradations Ltd, UK.
Printed and bound in China.

A CIP catalogue for this book is available from the British Library

ISBN 978-1-47111-084-9

1 2 3 4 5 6 7 8 9 10

Pictured on the title page: Grilled cod with a Caribbean salsa p78.
Pictured on the Introduction: Salmon and potato tart p162, Fish stew with saffron
p150, Thai style mussels p80.

WeightWatchers®

Simple, tasty fish and seafood recipes

Easy Fish

SIMON &
SCHUSTER
ILLUSTRATED

London · New York · Sydney · Toronto · New Delhi

A CBS COMPANY

Weight Watchers **ProPoints** Weight Loss System is a simple way to lose weight. As part of the Weight Watchers **ProPoints** plan you'll enjoy eating delicious, healthy, filling foods that help to keep you feeling satisfied for longer and in control of your portions.

⊙ This symbol denotes a vegetarian recipe and assumes that, where relevant, free range eggs, vegetarian cheese, vegetarian virtually fat free fromage frais, vegetarian low fat crème fraîche and vegetarian low fat yogurts are used. Virtually fat free fromage frais, low fat crème fraîche and low fat yogurts may contain traces of gelatine so they are not always vegetarian. Please check the labels.

❄ This symbol denotes a dish that can be frozen. Unless otherwise stated, you can freeze the finished dish for up to 3 months. Defrost thoroughly and reheat until the dish is piping hot throughout.

Recipe notes

Egg size: Medium sized, unless otherwise stated.

Raw eggs: Only the freshest eggs should be used. Pregnant women, the elderly and children should avoid recipes with eggs that are not fully cooked or raw.

All fruits and vegetables: Medium sized, unless otherwise stated.

Stock: Stock cubes are used in recipes, unless otherwise stated. These should be prepared according to packet instructions.

Recipe timings: These are approximate and meant to be guidelines. Please note that the preparation time includes all the steps up to and following the main cooking time(s).

Microwaves: Timings and temperatures are for a standard 800 W microwave. If necessary, adjust your own microwave.

Low fat spread: Where a recipe states to use a low fat spread, a light spread with a fat content of no less than 38% should be used.

Low fat soft cheese: Where low fat soft cheese is specified in a recipe, this refers to soft cheese with a fat content of less than 5%.

Contents

Introduction

Fish and seafood – ingredients that many people worry about cooking. Weight Watchers is here to help with this tasty collection of tried and tested recipes from the best of their cookbooks. All easy to prepare and cook, there are fish and seafood recipes here for every day and all occasions.

Try Tuna Melt Bagels for a tasty lunch with the family, rustle up Sweet and Sour Prawns instead of getting your usual takeaway or surprise a loved one with something special like Mexican Swordfish with Spicy Salsa. From traditional dishes such as Family Fish Pie to speedy ones like Seafood Kebabs, there is plenty here to excite your tastebuds.

So give fish and seafood a try. You might be surprised at how easy it is to cook and how delicious it can be.

About Weight Watchers

For more than 40 years Weight Watchers has been helping people around the world to lose weight using a long term sustainable approach. Weight Watchers successful weight loss system is based on four tried and trusted principles:

- Eating healthily
- Being more active
- Adjusting behaviour to help weight loss
- Getting support in weekly meetings

Our unique **ProPoints** system empowers you to manage your food plan and make wise recipe choices for a healthier, happier you.

To find out more about Weight Watchers and the **ProPoints** values for these recipes contact Customer Service on 0845 345 1500.

Buying fish and seafood

The best way to buy fresh fish and seafood is from a fishmonger, so get to know your local one. He or she will be able to tell you what is fresh in that day and what is in season. Large supermarkets usually have a fishmonger counter, or try farmer's markets or good street markets. You may even be lucky enough to have a fishmonger's shop in your town. Most fishmongers will be happy to recommend a fish and fillet it for you, so don't be afraid to ask.

Whole fish should have bright, clear eyes and the skin should be vibrant and shiny with no discolouration. The gills should be bright pink or red and wet, not slimy or dry. Fish fillets should be firm, moist and translucent. If the flesh looks flaky, dry or is separating from itself, avoid it. Fresh fish and seafood should smell of the sea and not fishy – if it smells fishy, don't buy it as it's not fresh.

If you don't have a fishmonger, look for frozen fish. This is usually frozen quickly and so will probably be fresher than packaged chilled fish. If you still cannot find what you want, remember that many of the recipes in this book can be adapted for other fish, especially those using firm white fish, so if you are looking for cod but can only find pollock, give it a try.

Storing and freezing

Fish and seafood is best cooked and eaten as soon as possible after buying it. It will keep for a couple of days in the fridge if wrapped well and sealed in a freezer bag or container, but will lose its freshness. So, if you can't cook it straight away, think about freezing it. However, it is important to make sure you know how to freeze safely.

- Wrap any food to be frozen in rigid containers or strong freezer bags. This is important to stop foods contaminating each other or getting freezer burn.
- Label the containers or bags with the contents and date – your freezer should have a star marking that tells you how long you can keep different types of frozen food.
- Never freeze warm food – always let it cool completely first.
- Never freeze food that has already been frozen and defrosted.
- Freeze food in portions, then you can take out as little or as much as you need each time.
- Defrost what you need in the fridge, making sure you put fish or seafood that might have juices on a covered plate or in a container.

Shopping hints and tips

Always buy the best ingredients you can afford. If you are going to cook healthy meals, it is worth investing in some quality ingredients that will really add flavour to your dishes.

When you're going around the supermarket it's tempting to pick up foods you like and put them in your trolley without thinking about how you will use them. So, a good plan is to decide what dishes you want to cook before you go shopping, check your store cupboard and make a list of what you need. You'll save time by not drifting aimlessly around the supermarket picking up what you fancy.

We've added a checklist here for some of the store cupboard ingredients used in this book. Just add fresh ingredients in your regular shop and you'll be ready to cook the wonderful recipes in *Easy Fish*.

Store cupboard checklist

- [ ] almonds, ground
- [ ] anchovies, in a jar
- [ ] apricots, dried
- [ ] bamboo shoots, canned
- [x] bay leaves
- [x] breadcrumbs, dried natural
- [ ] capers
- [ ] chick peas, canned
- [ ] chilli (flakes and powder)
- [ ] chilli sauce, sweet
- [x] Chinese five spice
- [ ] coconut milk, reduced fat
- [x] cooking spray, calorie controlled
- [x] coriander seeds
- [x] coriander, ground
- [x] cornflour
- [ ] couscous, dried
- [ ] crab meat, canned in brine

- [x] cumin seeds
- [x] cumin, ground
- [x] curry (paste and powder)
- [ ] fish sauce
- [x] flour, plain white
- [x] herbs, dried
- [ ] horseradish sauce
- [ ] lemongrass, ready prepared
- [ ] lentils, dried Puy
- [ ] mayonnaise, low fat
- [ ] mussels in a jar
- [x] mustard (English, Dijon and wholegrain)
- [ ] mustard seeds
- [ ] noodles, dried
- [x] oil (olive and vegetable)
- [ ] olives in brine, black
- [x] paprika
- [ ] passata
- [ ] pasta, dried
- [ ] peppercorns

- [ ] pineapple pieces, canned in natural juice
- [ ] rice, dried (brown, risotto and long grain)
- [x] saffron
- [x] salt
- [x] soy sauce
- [x] stock cubes (fish and vegetable)
- [x] sugar (light brown and caster)
- [ ] sweetcorn, canned
- [ ] Tabasco sauce
- [ ] tartare sauce
- [x] tomato ketchup
- [x] tomato purée
- [x] tomatoes, canned
- [ ] tuna, canned in brine
- [ ] turmeric
- [x] vinegar (balsamic, rice or white wine)
- [x] Worcestershire sauce

Light bites

Prawn noodle soup

Serves 4
175 calories per serving
Takes 25 minutes

90 g (3¼ oz) dried egg
  noodles, broken roughly
1 teaspoon olive oil
2 garlic cloves, crushed
1 cm (½ inch) fresh root
  ginger, chopped finely
4 spring onions, sliced finely
240 g (8½ oz) raw peeled king
  prawns
1.2 litres (2 pints) hot
  vegetable stock
1 small leek, sliced thinly
salt and freshly ground black
  pepper

This Oriental soup has a deliciously delicate and tasty flavour.

1 Bring a pan of water to the boil, add the noodles and simmer for 4 minutes or according to the packet instructions. Drain and set aside.

2 Heat the oil in a medium saucepan. Add the garlic, ginger and spring onions and stir-fry for 2–3 minutes.

3 Add the prawns and stir-fry for a further 1–2 minutes before adding the stock. Simmer for 2 minutes.

4 Add the noodles and leek to the pan and cook for a further 2–3 minutes. Check the seasoning and serve in four warmed bowls.

Variation... The prawns can be substituted for strips of lean pork – just stir-fry the pork for slightly longer before adding the stock.

Classic fish soup with rouille

Serves 6
250 calories per serving
Takes 30 minutes to prepare, 45 minutes to cook

*Enjoy this soup with a pungent garlic mayonnaise – a popular way to serve fish soup
all over the Mediterranean. This soup is quite an elaborate affair and ideal for a special
occasion.*

1 kg (2 lb 4 oz) mixed fresh white fish, filleted
  and heads and trimmings reserved (ask the
  fishmonger to include them)
250 g (9 oz) raw prawns in shells, defrosted if
  frozen, peeled and shells reserved
a small bunch of fresh parsley
1 bay leaf
2 onions, halved
a pinch of saffron (optional)
2 tablespoons boiling water (optional)
calorie controlled cooking spray
3 celery sticks, sliced

3 garlic cloves, crushed
400 g can chopped tomatoes
a strip of orange zest
1 tablespoon fennel seeds
1 tablespoon tomato purée
1 kg (2 lb 4 oz) fresh mussels, prepared
salt and freshly ground black pepper

For the rouille
2 garlic cloves, crushed
2 tablespoons low fat mayonnaise
juice of ½ a lemon

1 Put the fish trimmings and prawn shells in a large lidded saucepan. Cover with 1.5 litres
(2¾ pints) of water and add the parsley stalks, bay leaf and half an onion. Season, bring to the boil
and simmer for 15 minutes. Strain and set aside, throwing away the shells and trimmings. Place
the saffron in the boiling water to soak, if using.

2 Heat a large, lidded, non stick saucepan, spray with the cooking spray and stir-fry the remaining
onion halves and the celery for 5 minutes until softened. Add a little water if necessary to prevent
the mixture from sticking.

continues overleaf ▶

3 Stir in the garlic, tomatoes, orange zest, fennel seeds, tomato purée and saffron with its soaking liquid, if using. Season to taste, add the strained fish stock and bring to the boil. Cover and simmer for 20 minutes.

4 Meanwhile, make the rouille by stirring together the garlic and mayonnaise with the lemon juice and seasoning.

5 Add the fish to the soup and cook for 1 minute, then add the mussels and prawns. Boil for another 4–5 minutes until the fish is opaque, the prawns pink and all the mussels are open, discarding any that remain closed.

6 Chop the remaining parsley and scatter over the soup. Serve with a swirl of rouille on top of each serving.

Tips... Step 1 results in a delicious fish stock that can be used as a base for many fish soups and dishes, but you can always use bought fish stock instead.

To prepare mussels, scrub off any dirt and remove any barnacles. Remove the beard, if any, that sticks out between the shells. Discard any mussels that are already open or have a cracked shell.

Mussel and tomato chowder

Serves 4

225 calories per serving

Takes 10 minutes to prepare,
25 minutes to cook

**calorie controlled cooking
spray**

**4 lean back bacon rashers,
diced finely**

1 large onion, chopped finely

1 celery stick, chopped finely

**1 carrot, peeled and chopped
finely**

1.2 litres (2 pints) fish stock

**2 potatoes, peeled and cut into
1 cm (½ inch) dice**

**2 x 400 g cans chopped
tomatoes**

**2 x 205 g jars mussels,
drained and rinsed**

**a small bunch of fresh thyme,
woody stems removed and
leaves chopped**

**salt and freshly ground black
pepper**

This is a delicious and satisfying soup.

1 Heat a large, lidded, non stick saucepan, spray with the
cooking spray and stir-fry the bacon for 2 minutes until it
begins to brown. Add the onion, celery and carrot, season,
cover and cook for about 10 minutes until soft, adding a little of
the stock if necessary to prevent the mixture from sticking.

2 Add the potatoes, tomatoes and remaining stock and bring
to the boil. Simmer for 10 minutes and then add the mussels
and thyme and simmer gently for 2 minutes more. Check that
the potatoes are tender, season to taste and serve.

Variation... Fresh mussels (1 kg/2 lb 4 oz) could be used
instead of the canned ones, but wash them very well first
(see Tip on opposite page). Add with the stock and discard
any that have not opened after simmering.

Smoked trout couscous salad

Serves 2
246 calories per serving
Takes 10 minutes

100 g (3½ oz) dried couscous
150 ml (5 fl oz) boiling water
6 radishes, sliced into half
   moons
200 g (7 oz) cucumber, diced
1 spring onion, sliced
50 g (1¾ oz) watercress,
   washed
125 g (4½ oz) smoked trout
   fillets, flaked
salt and freshly ground black
   pepper

For the dressing
80 g (3 oz) low fat natural
   yogurt
2 teaspoons horseradish
   sauce

Smoked trout has a delicate flavour and texture that is complemented by the kick of the horseradish dressing.

1 Tip the couscous into a bowl, season and pour over the boiling water. Stir, cover and leave to stand for 5 minutes. Stir the radishes, cucumber and spring onion into the softened couscous.

2 To make the dressing, mix the yogurt and horseradish sauce together and season.

3 Divide the watercress between two bowls and pile the couscous on top. Add the smoked trout and drizzle with the dressing just before serving.

Crab coleslaw

Serves 4

180 calories per serving

Takes 20 minutes

2 x 170 g cans white crab meat in brine

½ red onion, sliced finely

1 apple, cored and sliced finely

150 g (5½ oz) white cabbage, shredded finely

75 g (2¾ oz) cucumber, sliced finely

25 g packet fresh coriander, chopped roughly

1 small carrot, peeled and grated

1 avocado, peeled, stoned and sliced thinly

salt and freshly ground black pepper

For the dressing

grated zest and juice of 2 limes

4 tablespoons virtually fat free plain fromage frais

1 teaspoon tomato purée

a few drops of Tabasco

½ teaspoon Worcestershire sauce

Simple but full of flavour, this is perfect for a quick lunch.

1 In a bowl, mix together all the dressing ingredients and season. Set aside.

2 Drain one can of crab meat and empty into a large bowl. Mix in the onion, apple, cabbage, cucumber, coriander and carrot.

3 Add the dressing and toss gently to combine. Divide the avocado between four plates and top each with a generous amount of the crab coleslaw. Drain the remaining can of crab meat and crumble over the top of each salad.

Herring Caesar salad

Serves 4
352 calories per serving
Takes 20 minutes

2 Romaine lettuce hearts,
  cored and sliced thickly
125 g (4½ oz) cucumber,
  sliced thinly
3 celery sticks, sliced thickly
5 tablespoons low fat Caesar
  dressing
1 avocado, peeled, stoned and
  cubed
50 g (1¾ oz) grated Parmesan
  cheese
1 egg white
50 g (1¾ oz) fresh white
  breadcrumbs
1 teaspoon mild chilli powder
3 x 100 g (3½ oz) herring
  cutlets or fillets
calorie controlled cooking
  spray
1 lemon, cut into wedges, to
  serve

These little fish are available from the fish counter in most supermarkets or fishmongers.

1 Put the lettuce, cucumber and celery in a large salad bowl. Lightly toss with half the dressing. Divide between four plates and top with the avocado. Drizzle with the remaining dressing and scatter over the Parmesan cheese.

2 In a shallow, clean, grease-free bowl, lightly whisk the egg white. Put the breadcrumbs and chilli powder into another shallow bowl. Cut each herring fillet in half and then in half again to make 12 pieces. Dip the pieces, skin side only, into the egg white and then into the breadcrumbs until the skin is coated.

3 Heat a non stick frying pan and spray the fillets with the cooking spray. Breadcrumb side down, cook the fillets gently for 2 minutes until golden and then turn over and cook for another 2–3 minutes until cooked. Serve three pieces of herring on top of each salad with the lemon wedges on the side.

Mackerel pâté

Serves 2
201 calories per serving
Takes 5 minutes

75 g (2¾ oz) smoked mackerel fillets
40 g (1½ oz) low fat soft cheese
2 tablespoons 0% fat Greek yogurt
2 teaspoons finely chopped fresh dill
salt and freshly ground black pepper

To serve
4 wholewheat crispbreads
snipped fresh chives
a few sprigs of watercress, washed

This quick and easy spread is great served on wholewheat crispbreads with a little watercress on the side.

1 Flake the mackerel into a small bowl.

2 Add the soft cheese, yogurt and dill. Mix well. Taste and then season.

3 Serve on top of the crispbreads, garnished with chives and accompanied by sprigs of watercress.

Tips... Try adding a ½ teaspoon of lemon zest for extra flavour.

If you can't find dill, try 1 tablespoon of chopped fresh parsley. 1 small chopped spring onion works well too.

Fluffy tuna jackets

Serves 2

270 calories per serving

Takes 15 minutes to prepare,
1¼ hours to cook

❄

**2 x 225 g (8 oz) baking
potatoes**

**100 g (3½ oz) canned tuna in
brine, drained and flaked**

**50 g (1¾ oz) low fat soft
cheese**

**50 g (1¾ oz) canned or frozen
and drefrosted sweetcorn**

1 egg white

**salt and freshly ground black
pepper**

A great way to fill baked potatoes, everyone will love these.

1 Preheat the oven to Gas Mark 6/200°C/fan oven 180°C.

2 Prick the potatoes all over. Bake them for 1 hour until they
are tender. Slice them in half and, using a small teaspoon,
carefully scoop out the flesh into a small bowl. Reserve the
potato skins.

3 Add the tuna, soft cheese and sweetcorn to the potato
flesh, season and stir well.

4 In a clean, grease-free bowl, whisk the egg white until it
forms stiff peaks. Fold it into the potato and tuna mixture.
Spoon the mixture into the potato shells and then return them
to the oven for 15 minutes to heat through.

Tuna, sweetcorn and caper mini pizzas

Serves 4

335 calories per serving

Takes 10 minutes to prepare,
10–15 minutes to cook

4 x 10 cm (4 inch) pizza bases
4 tablespoons passata
200 g can sweetcorn, drained
200 g can tuna in brine,
drained
juice of a lemon
1 tablespoon olive oil
2 tablespoons capers, drained
salt and freshly ground black
pepper

These mini pizzas are delicious with ready-made or home-made dough.

1 Preheat the oven to Gas Mark 9/240°C/fan oven 220°C. Spread the top of each pizza base with a tablespoon of the passata.

2 In a bowl, mix together the sweetcorn and tuna with the lemon juice and olive oil and then pile on top of the pizzas. Finish with the capers and seasoning.

3 Bake for 10–15 minutes or until the pizza crusts are crisp and golden.

Tuna and broccoli quiche

Serves 4

395 calories per serving

Takes 35 minutes to prepare +
20 minutes chilling,
45–50 minutes to cook

❄

For the pastry

**150 g (5½ oz) plain white flour,
plus 2 teaspoons for rolling**

15 g (½ oz) cornflour

75 g (2¾ oz) low fat spread

a pinch of salt

For the filling

150 g (5½ oz) broccoli florets

**185 g can tuna in brine,
drained and flaked**

2 eggs

300 ml (10 fl oz) skimmed milk

**salt and freshly ground black
pepper**

Serve this filling quiche with a crisp mixed salad.

1 To make the pastry, sift the flour and cornflour into a mixing bowl. Using your fingertips, rub in the low fat spread until the mixture resembles fine breadcrumbs. Add a pinch of salt and enough cold water to make a soft dough.

2 Roll out the pastry on a lightly floured surface and use it to line a 20 cm (8 inch) loose-bottomed, fluted flan tin. Chill the pastry in the fridge for 20 minutes.

3 Preheat the oven to Gas Mark 6/200°C/fan oven 180°C. Line the pastry case with non stick baking parchment and baking beans and bake blind for 10 minutes. Remove the paper and the beans and return the flan tin to the oven for 5 minutes.

4 Meanwhile, bring a pan of water to the boil, add the broccoli, cook for 5 minutes and then drain well. Arrange the broccoli and the tuna in the partially baked pastry case. Reduce the oven temperature to Gas Mark 4/180°C/fan oven 160°C.

5 Whisk together the eggs and milk with a little seasoning and pour the mixture over the broccoli and tuna. Put the flan on a baking tray and return it to the oven for 45–50 minutes, until the filling has set. Serve warm or cold.

Smoked fish ramekins

Serves 6

130 calories per serving

Takes 15 minutes to prepare,
15–20 minutes to cook

calorie controlled cooking spray

250 g (9 oz) skinless smoked haddock fillet, cut into chunks

75 g (2¾ oz) smoked salmon, snipped into tiny pieces

100 g (3½ oz) low fat soft cheese

4 eggs, beaten

200 ml (7 fl oz) skimmed milk

1 tablespoon chopped fresh chives, parsley or spring onions

freshly ground black pepper

6 medium slices wholemeal bread, to serve

You can serve these ramekins cold as a spread and they're ideal as a packed lunch too.

1 Preheat the oven to Gas Mark 4/180°C/fan oven 160°C. Spray six ramekin dishes or individual baking dishes with the cooking spray.

2 Mix together the haddock and salmon and share the mixture between the prepared dishes. Place the dishes on a baking tray.

3 Tip the soft cheese into a bowl and beat with a wooden spoon to soften it. Whisk in the eggs and milk to make a smooth mixture and then stir in the chives, parsley or spring onions. Season with a little black pepper; you won't need any salt. Pour an equal amount of the mixture into each dish.

4 Bake in the oven for 15–20 minutes until set. Leave to cool for a few minutes. Meanwhile, toast the bread and cut in half. Serve with the fish.

Chinese style scrambled eggs

Serves 2
215 calories per serving
Takes 15 minutes

1 teaspoon sunflower oil
4 spring onions, sliced
100 g (3½ oz) beansprouts
3 eggs
3 tablespoons skimmed milk
1 tablespoon light soy sauce
50 g (1¾ oz) cooked peeled prawns

A twist on plain scrambled eggs, try serving this tasty snack on a medium slice of toast.

1 Heat the sunflower oil in a small non stick saucepan and add the spring onions and beansprouts. Stir-fry for 2 minutes until they begin to soften.

2 Beat together the eggs, milk and soy sauce and add the mixture to the pan with the prawns. Cook, stirring continuously, until the eggs begin to scramble. This will take about 5 minutes. Serve immediately.

Spring rolls

Serves 4

265 calories per serving

Takes 25 minutes to prepare,
10 minutes to cook

calorie controlled cooking
spray

100 g (3½ oz) carrots, peeled
and sliced into thin strips

100 g (3½ oz) white cabbage,
shredded

1 small red pepper, de-seeded
and sliced thinly

100 g (3½ oz) cooked peeled
prawns

100 g (3½ oz) beansprouts

2 tablespoons dark soy sauce,
plus extra for dipping

¼ teaspoon Chinese five spice

8 x 15 g (½ oz) sheets filo
pastry, measuring
30 x 40 cm (12 x 16 inches)

2 tablespoons sunflower oil

These tasty, crunchy vegetable and prawn rolls have all the flavour of those served in Chinese restaurants, but they are far healthier since they are baked and not deep fried.

1 To make the filling, spray a large non stick frying pan with the cooking spray. Add the carrots, cabbage, pepper, prawns, beansprouts, soy sauce and Chinese five spice and stir-fry for 2 minutes. Remove the pan from the heat and allow the mixture to cool a little.

2 Preheat the oven to Gas Mark 5/190°C/fan oven 170°C. Line a baking tray with non stick baking parchment.

3 Brush a sheet of filo pastry with a little of the oil. Spoon some of the filling on to one end of the pastry sheet and roll the pastry up, tucking in the edges to enclose the filling so that you end up with a sausage shape. Repeat this process with the remaining pastry sheets until you have eight spring rolls.

4 Place the spring rolls on the baking tray and bake for 10 minutes until they are golden and crispy. Serve them hot with extra soy sauce for dipping, allowing two spring rolls per person.

Smoked salmon mousse with cucumber and dill relish

Serves 4

150 calories per serving

Takes 15 minutes + chilling

❄ (mousse only)

For the mousse

150 g (5½ oz) smoked salmon

finely grated zest of a lemon

2 tablespoons lemon juice

1 tablespoon horseradish sauce

200 g (7 oz) low fat soft cheese

1 teaspoon powdered gelatine

salt and freshly ground black pepper

For the relish

225 g (8 oz) cucumber

1 tablespoon chopped fresh dill

1 tablespoon white wine vinegar

1 tablespoon caster sugar

So easy and delicious. When entertaining guests, serve this as a starter and no one will ever know it's a Weight Watchers dish.

1 For the mousse, snip the salmon into small pieces and place in a food processor with the lemon zest, lemon juice, horseradish sauce and soft cheese. Blend until smooth and then transfer to a mixing bowl.

2 Place 2 tablespoons of cold water in a small bowl. Sprinkle the gelatine over and leave to stand for 5 minutes until it looks spongy. Place over a pan of gently simmering water and heat for about 2 minutes until the gelatine mixture goes clear and runny. Remove from the heat and beat into the salmon mixture. Season to taste and then transfer to a suitable container and chill for at least 2 hours.

3 For the relish, peel the cucumber and slice in half lengthways. Use a small spoon to scoop the seeds out. Slice the cucumber as thinly as you can. You can use the slicing side of a grater for this job. Transfer to a bowl and toss with the dill, vinegar and sugar. Chill until required.

4 To serve, arrange some of the cucumber relish on individual serving plates and top with a scoopful of smoked salmon mousse.

Tip... Most deli counters sell smoked salmon pieces, which are a lot cheaper than sliced smoked salmon and perfect to use in this recipe.

Red hot prawn pittas

Serves 2
250 calories per serving
Takes 7 minutes

2 pitta breads
calorie controlled cooking spray
½ red onion, sliced thinly
100 g (3½ oz) stir-fry vegetables
½ red pepper, de-seeded and sliced thinly
75 g (2¾ oz) cooked peeled prawns, defrosted if frozen
1½ tablespoons sweet chilli sauce
salt and freshly ground black pepper

Adapt these to suit your taste by adding a little more or less of the chilli sauce.

1 Heat a wok or non stick frying pan until very hot. At the same time, warm the pitta breads in a toaster or under the grill.

2 Spray the wok or frying pan with the cooking spray, add the onion and stir-fry for a few seconds. Add the stir-fry vegetables and pepper and cook for another minute or two, stirring all the time.

3 Add the prawns and stir-fry for another few moments to heat through. Stir in the chilli sauce, season and then stuff into the warmed pitta breads. Serve at once.

Ⓥ **Variation...** For a vegetarian version, omit the prawns and use 75 g (2¾ oz) drained canned chick peas instead.

Tuna melt bagels

Serves 4
342 calories per serving
Takes 15 minutes

4 medium bagels, split
200 g can tuna in brine, drained
4 spring onions, chopped
75 g (2¾ oz) 0% fat Greek yogurt
60 g (2 oz) half fat Cheddar cheese, grated
4 tomatoes, sliced
freshly ground black pepper

An American classic that is ideal served with a crisp mixed salad.

1 Preheat the grill to medium high and lightly toast the bagels on both sides.

2 Meanwhile, in a bowl, flake in the tuna and mix with the spring onions, yogurt and cheese. Season to taste with black pepper.

3 Divide up the tomato slices and place on top of the cut sides of the bagels. Spoon the tuna mixture on top. Grill for 3–4 minutes until golden and bubbling and serve immediately.

King prawn, red onion and pepper bruschetta

Serves 2

266 calories per serving

Takes 15 minutes to prepare,
20–25 minutes to cook

1 red onion, halved and cut
  into half rings

1 small red pepper, de-seeded
  and diced

1 small green pepper,
  de-seeded and diced

1 tablespoon olive oil

1 garlic clove, crushed

1 teaspoon balsamic vinegar

1 fresh thyme sprig

100 g (3½ oz) cooked peeled
  king prawns

15 cm (6 inch) French stick,
  halved horizontally

1 tablespoon sun-dried tomato
  purée

salt and freshly ground black
  pepper

Roasted vegetables give these bruschetta a rich flavour.

1 Preheat the oven to Gas Mark 6/200°C/fan oven 180°C. Line a roasting tin with non stick baking parchment.

2 In a bowl, toss the onion, peppers, olive oil, garlic and vinegar together and then put them in the roasting tin with the thyme sprig. Roast for 20–25 minutes, turning occasionally, until tender and beginning to char at the edges. Add the prawns to the vegetables for the last 5 minutes of the cooking time.

3 Toast the French stick halves on one side until golden and then spread them with the tomato purée. Top with the roasted vegetables and prawns and season to taste.

Family favourites

Tuna pasta bake

Serves 4
420 calories per serving
Takes 25 minutes
❄

250 g (9 oz) dried pasta
   shapes
1 onion, chopped
400 ml (14 fl oz) skimmed milk
2 tablespoons cornflour
100 g (3½ oz) frozen peas,
   defrosted
200 g can tuna in brine,
   drained and flaked
50 g (1¾ oz) half fat Cheddar
   cheese, grated
15 g (½ oz) Parmesan cheese,
   grated
2 tablespoons dried natural
   breadcrumbs
6–8 cherry tomatoes, halved
salt and freshly ground black
   pepper

*A great family favourite from America, this quick budget
dish is bound to please everyone, and the all-in-one sauce
is so easy to make – fantastic.*

1 Bring a large pan of water to the boil, add the pasta and
onion and cook according to the packet instructions. Drain,
rinse in cold water and set aside.

2 Meanwhile, make the sauce. In a heatproof jug, mix
3 tablespoons of the milk with the cornflour to make a smooth
paste. In a large saucepan, put the rest of the milk on to boil.
When the liquid starts to creep up the sides of the pan, pour it
over the cornflour paste, whisking as you do so.

3 Return the milk mixture to the pan and cook, stirring, on
a low heat until it thickens. Add the peas and tuna and then
simmer for 2 minutes. Remove the pan from the heat and set
aside to cool slightly.

4 Mix in all the Cheddar cheese and half of the Parmesan.
Stir the cooked pasta and onion into the sauce and check the
seasoning. Reheat it all gently in the pan but do not allow it to
boil. Preheat the grill.

5 Transfer the pasta mixture to a flameproof dish. Mix the
remaining Parmesan with the breadcrumbs and scatter over
the top. Arrange the tomato halves, cut side up, over the
breadcrumb topping. Place the dish under the grill and cook
until the top is crispy and golden.

Fish goujons with tartare sauce

Serves 6
201 calories per serving
Takes 35 minutes

50 g (1¾ oz) plain white flour
½ teaspoon chilli powder
2 large egg whites, beaten
300 g (10½ oz) fresh white breadcrumbs
100 g (3½ oz) skinless plaice fillet, cut into thick strips
salt
lemon wedges, to serve

For the tartare sauce
100 g (3½ oz) low fat soft cheese
200 ml (7 fl oz) virtually fat free plain fromage frais
2 tablespoons capers, rinsed and squeezed to remove excess vinegar
4 small gherkins, chopped finely
2 spring onions, chopped finely
a small bunch of fresh dill or fennel, chopped
freshly ground black pepper

Serve these crisp coated fish pieces as finger food, with the creamy tartare sauce as a dip.

1 Preheat the grill to a medium heat. Mix the flour, chilli powder and a little salt together in a shallow bowl. Place the egg whites in a second bowl and the breadcrumbs in a third one. Dip some of the fish strips first in the chilli flour, then in the egg whites and finally in the breadcrumbs. Spread out on a grill pan lined with foil.

2 Grill the goujons until golden and crisp and cooked through, turning over once or twice to brown all over. Repeat with the remaining fish strips.

3 Meanwhile, make the tartare sauce by beating together the soft cheese and fromage frais and then stirring in all the other ingredients with some seasoning. Tip into a serving bowl and serve with the goujons, with the lemon wedges to squeeze over.

Baked haddock with tomatoes

Serves 4

265 calories per serving

Takes 40 minutes to prepare,
   35–40 minutes to cook

800 g (1 lb 11 oz) potatoes,
   peeled and cut into chunks

calorie controlled cooking
   spray

2 onions, sliced thinly

2 garlic cloves, sliced thinly

400 g (14 oz) haddock fillets,
   skin left on

400 g can chopped tomatoes

1 tablespoon balsamic vinegar
   or lemon juice

salt and freshly ground black
   pepper

a handful of chopped fresh
   parsley, to garnish (optional)

*A quick, no-hassle recipe that, except for the fish, you will
probably have all the ingredients for in your storecupboard.*

1 Bring a pan of water to the boil, add the potatoes and cook
until soft, about 25 minutes. Drain.

2 Meanwhile, preheat the oven to Gas Mark 3/170°C/fan oven
150°C. Heat a non stick frying pan, spray with the cooking spray
and fry the onions and garlic for 4 minutes until softened.

3 Spray an ovenproof dish with the cooking spray and put the
fish fillets in, skin side down. Scatter the onions and garlic over
the top, pour over the tomatoes, vinegar and 125 ml (4 fl oz) of
water and season well. Bake for 35–40 minutes.

4 To serve, mash the potatoes, season and spoon on to four
plates. Top with a piece of fish and some of the sauce. Garnish
with the chopped parsley, if using.

Variation... You could serve the haddock with 60 g (2 oz)
dried pasta or 100 g (3½ oz) dried couscous per person,
cooked according to the packet instructions, instead of the
potatoes.

Fish and chips

Serves 4

415 calories per serving

Takes 10 minutes to prepare, 20 minutes to cook

For the chips

1 vegetable stock cube

900 g (2 lb) potatoes, peeled and cut into chips

1½ tablespoons vegetable oil

salt

For the fish

1 egg, beaten

2 tablespoons skimmed milk

75 g (2¾ oz) fresh white breadcrumbs

¼ teaspoon turmeric

4 x 150 g (5½ oz) skinless haddock fillets

calorie controlled cooking spray

salt and freshly ground black pepper

Take-away chips might be delicious, but they are usually cooked in fat. With these scrumptious home-made chips, you get a generously sized portion that is much healthier.

1 Preheat the oven to Gas Mark 6/200°C/fan oven 180°C.

2 Bring a large lidded pan of water to the boil, add the stock cube and tip in the chips. Cover and cook for 5 minutes until just tender. Drain the chips into a colander.

3 Beat the egg with the milk and some seasoning and then pour into a shallow dish. Mix the breadcrumbs and turmeric together and spread out on a plate. Pat the fish dry on kitchen towel and then dip each piece first in the egg and then in the breadcrumbs to coat. Place on a non stick baking tray and spray lightly with the cooking spray.

4 Carefully toss the chips in the oil and spread them out on a large non stick baking tray. Sprinkle with salt and place on the top shelf of the oven. Cook for 5 minutes and then add the tray of fish to the oven and cook both for 15 minutes.

5 Serve up the fish and chips on warmed serving plates.

Puttanesca pasta

Serves 4
214 calories per serving
Takes 25 minutes
❄ (sauce only)

175 g (6 oz) dried tagliatelle
1 teaspoon vegetable oil
50 g (1¾ oz) anchovies, rinsed and chopped roughly
2 garlic cloves, crushed
10 black olives in brine, drained, stoned and halved
2 tablespoons capers, drained
400 g can chopped tomatoes
1 tablespoon chopped fresh oregano leaves, plus extra to garnish (optional), or 2 teaspoons dried oregano
salt and freshly ground black pepper

This classic pasta sauce was once made by 'ladies of the night' to woo customers.

1 Bring a large pan of water to the boil, add the pasta and cook for 10–12 minutes or according to the packet instructions. Drain and rinse thoroughly.

2 Meanwhile, heat the oil in a non stick saucepan, add the anchovies and cook, stirring, over a medium heat for 3 minutes. Add the garlic and cook for a further 3 minutes until the anchovies have virtually dissolved.

3 Add the olives, capers, tomatoes and oregano. Bring to the boil, reduce the heat and simmer for 5 minutes until thick. Season to taste.

4 Pour the sauce over the pasta and toss to mix. Garnish with extra oregano leaves, if using.

Fabulous fish cakes

Serves 4

255 calories per serving

Takes 20 minutes to prepare,
30–35 minutes to cook

❄

225 g (8 oz) skinless smoked
haddock fillet

225 g (8 oz) skinless cod fillet

450 g (1 lb) cold mashed
potato

4 spring onions, chopped
finely

2 teaspoons Thai red or green
curry paste (optional)

1 small egg, beaten

75 g (2¾ oz) canned or frozen
and defrosted sweetcorn

3 tablespoons plain white
flour

salt and freshly ground black
pepper

a few fresh chives or shredded
spring onions, to garnish

a handful of mixed salad
leaves, to serve

*You could also serve these with stir-fried vegetables,
seasoned with a few drops of soy sauce and chilli sauce.*

1 Put the fish fillets in a large frying pan and pour in enough
cold water just to cover them. Poach gently for 5–6 minutes,
until the flesh looks opaque and flakes easily when tested with
a fork.

2 Lift the fish from the frying pan and flake the flesh roughly.
Allow to cool completely.

3 Preheat the oven to Gas Mark 5/190°C/fan oven 170°C.
Put the potato in a large bowl and mix in the spring onions,
red or green curry paste, if using, egg and sweetcorn. Add the
fish, season and mix together gently. Form the mixture into
eight fish cakes and dust them with the flour.

4 Place the fish cakes on non stick baking trays and bake
them in the oven for 30–35 minutes, until brown. Allow two fish
cakes per person, garnished with chives or spring onions and
served with mixed salad leaves.

Tip... The Thai red or green curry paste gives the fish cakes
an extra kick – though you can leave it out if you prefer.

Variations... Try using 3 tablespoons of polenta instead of
flour for coating the fish cakes – it gives them a slightly
crunchier finish.

For a tasty shortcut, replace the fresh fish with canned
tuna. Use 2 x 200 g cans of tuna in brine or water,
thoroughly drained.

Cod in parsley sauce

Serves 4
280 calories per serving
Takes 40 minutes

600 ml (20 fl oz) skimmed milk

a large bunch of fresh parsley, leaves separated from stalks, chopped finely

2 tablespoons low fat spread

4 tablespoons plain white flour

1 teaspoon Dijon or wholegrain mustard

calorie controlled cooking spray

4 x 150 g (5½ oz) skinless cod fillets

salt and freshly ground black pepper

4 lemon wedges, to serve (optional)

This classic British sauce goes well with any fish. Serve each portion with 100 g (3½ oz) minted new potatoes and 2 heaped tablespoons of peas. Mange tout and baby corn are also delicious on the side.

1 Heat the milk with the parsley stalks until it's nearly boiling, then strain. Melt the low fat spread on a low heat in a medium non stick saucepan. Add the flour and stir until it becomes a ball of thick paste.

2 Add the milk a bit at a time, stirring vigorously after each addition until you have a thick, smooth paste. Keep adding the milk, stirring until the sauce is smooth and thick. If it looks lumpy at any point, just stop adding milk and continue to heat and stir vigorously until it is smooth again.

3 Stir the chopped parsley and mustard into the milk sauce and season. Turn off the heat.

4 Preheat the grill to medium. Set the cod fillets on the grill pan on a piece of foil sprayed with the cooking spray. Season the fillets and grill for 5–6 minutes until just cooked through, turning once and seasoning again.

5 Put the fillets on serving plates. Serve with the parsley sauce poured over and lemon wedges, if using.

Seafood spaghetti

Serves 4

480 calories per serving

Takes 20 minutes to prepare,
20 minutes to cook

350 g (12 oz) dried spaghetti

calorie controlled cooking
spray

2 onions, chopped

2 garlic cloves, crushed

1 red chilli, de-seeded and
chopped finely (optional)

400 g (14 oz) seafood
selection, defrosted if frozen

100 ml (3½ fl oz) white wine

2 tablespoons Worcestershire
sauce

1 teaspoon caster sugar

2 x 400 g cans chopped
tomatoes

4 tablespoons capers, drained

salt and freshly ground black
pepper

a small bunch of fresh basil,
to garnish

Take advantage of cooked frozen seafood in this easy dish.

1 Bring a pan of water to the boil, add the pasta and cook according to the packet instructions.

2 Meanwhile, spray a large non stick frying pan with the cooking spray and fry the onions, garlic and chilli, if using, over a medium heat for 5 minutes until the onions are softened. Add a splash of water if necessary to prevent them from sticking.

3 Add the seafood, wine, Worcestershire sauce, sugar, tomatoes and capers, season and stir together. Bring to the boil and then simmer for 20 minutes or until the sauce has thickened.

4 Drain the pasta, reserving about 4 tablespoons of the cooking liquid. Toss the pasta with the sauce and cooking liquid, sprinkle with the basil and serve.

Saffron seafood risotto

Serves 2

356 calories per serving

Takes 10 minutes to prepare,
35 minutes to cook

**calorie controlled cooking
spray**

3 garlic cloves, crushed

3 leeks, sliced finely

**1 red pepper, de-seeded and
diced**

**½ teaspoon fennel seeds,
crushed or ground**

250 g (9 oz) dried brown rice

**a good pinch of saffron
strands**

**1.2 litres (2 pints) fish,
chicken or vegetable stock**

**400 g (14 oz) seafood
selection, defrosted if frozen**

**a bunch of fresh parsley,
chopped**

**a few fresh dill sprigs,
chopped**

freshly ground black pepper

lemon wedges, to serve

Prepared in just one pot, this couldn't be easier to make.

1 Spray a large lidded pan with the cooking spray and stir-fry the garlic, leeks and pepper with 100 ml (3½ fl oz) of water for 5 minutes, or until softened.

2 Add the fennel seeds, rice and saffron and stir, then add the stock and stir again. Cover the pan and leave on a low heat for 30 minutes, or until nearly all the stock has been absorbed.

3 Add the seafood and fresh herbs and stir through. Replace the lid and cook for a further 5 minutes, or until the seafood is heated through. Season with black pepper and serve with lemon wedges.

Tip... If you don't have saffron strands, use a teaspoon of turmeric instead.

Variation... For a vegetarian version, replace the seafood selection with 200 g (7 oz) frozen peas.

Seafood kebabs

Serves 4
309 calories per serving
Takes 20 minutes

450 g (1 lb) skinless cod
    fillets, cut into 2.5 cm
    (1 inch) chunks
300 g (10½ oz) skinless
    salmon fillets, cut into
    2.5 cm (1 inch) chunks
2 garlic cloves, crushed
1½ tablespoons hot chilli
    sauce
juice of a lime
16 cherry tomatoes
1 lime, cut into 8 wedges
chopped fresh coriander, to
    garnish

These kebabs are perfect for cooking on the barbecue on a hot summer's day.

1 Soak four long (or eight short) wooden skewers in water for 10 minutes.

2 Place all the fish in a plastic bag. Mix together the garlic, chilli sauce and lime juice and add this to the bag. Holding the bag firmly closed, gently shake it to coat the fish with the marinade.

3 Preheat the grill to a medium heat or ensure your barbecue is ready. Divide the cod, salmon, tomatoes and lime wedges into four (or eight) groups and thread on to the skewers, alternating the ingredients.

4 Cook the kebabs for 3–4 minutes on each side, brushing with any remaining marinade. When the fish becomes opaque it is cooked. Serve hot, garnished with the coriander.

Kedgeree

Serves 4
335 calories per serving
Takes 25 minutes

200 g (7 oz) dried long grain rice
2 tablespoons medium curry powder
2 eggs
400 g (14 oz) skinless smoked haddock fillets
300 ml (10 fl oz) fish or vegetable stock
garlic calorie controlled cooking spray
1 onion, chopped
2 tablespoons chopped fresh parsley
salt and freshly ground black pepper
2 tomatoes, each cut into 6 wedges, to garnish

This makes a wonderful starter for six or an excellent weekend breakfast for four.

1 Put the rice and curry powder in a lidded pan and cover with water. Bring to the boil, cover and simmer for 10 minutes.

2 Meanwhile, bring another small pan of water to the boil, add the eggs and simmer for 8 minutes to hard boil. When the eggs are cooked, plunge into cold water to cool and then remove the shells.

3 Place the haddock and stock in a large lidded frying pan, cover and cook for 6 minutes (until the fish flakes easily).

4 Spray a non stick pan with the cooking spray and cook the onion until just starting to brown.

5 Flake the cooked fish. Cut the eggs into wedges. Drain the rice if necessary and then stir in a tablespoon of chopped parsley, the onion and flaked fish. Season to taste.

6 Divide the kedgeree between four serving plates, top with wedges of egg and sprinkle with the remaining parsley. Garnish with the tomato wedges and serve immediately.

Smoked haddock fish balls

Serves 4
195 calories per serving
Takes 40 minutes
❄

450 g (1 lb) potatoes, peeled
and diced

350 g (12 oz) skinless smoked
haddock fillet

4 tablespoons skimmed milk

2 teaspoons wholegrain
mustard

15 g packet low fat ready
salted crisps, crushed

calorie controlled cooking
spray

salt and freshly ground black
pepper

Wholegrain mustard goes particularly well with smoked fish; it certainly livens up these tasty fish balls.

1 Preheat the oven to Gas Mark 6/200°C/fan oven 180°C.

2 Bring a pan of water to the boil, add the potatoes and cook for 12–15 minutes until tender. Drain thoroughly and mash. Set aside.

3 Meanwhile, place the fish in a large lidded saucepan with the milk and 4 tablespoons of water and bring to the boil. Cover and simmer for 5 minutes until the fish flakes easily. Drain, reserving the liquid, and carefully flake the fish.

4 Place the mashed potatoes in a large mixing bowl. Add the flaked fish, 3 tablespoons of the reserved cooking liquid and the mustard. Season. Mix it all together thoroughly and then shape the mixture into eight small balls with your hands.

5 Line a baking tray with non stick baking parchment. Roll the balls in the crushed crisps and arrange them on the baking tray. Spray with the cooking spray and bake in the oven for 15 minutes. Serve hot.

Tip... Try making this delicious dip to serve with the haddock balls: mix 4 tablespoons of virtually fat free plain fromage frais with 1 de-seeded, skinned and finely diced tomato and 1 teaspoon of finely chopped fresh chives. Season and chill the dip until you need it.

Cod Kiev

Serves 4

195 calories per serving

Takes 15 minutes to prepare,
  20 minutes to cook

✳

**4 x 175 g (6 oz) skinless thick
  cod fillets**

**50 g (1¾ oz) low fat soft
  cheese with garlic and herbs**

1 egg, beaten

1 teaspoon dried parsley

**50 g (1¾ oz) fresh white
  breadcrumbs**

**calorie controlled cooking
  spray**

**salt and freshly ground black
  pepper**

*Calorie controlled cooking sprays are widely available
and you'll find them next to the other cooking oils. They
generally have only 1 calorie per spray.*

1 Preheat the oven to Gas Mark 6/200°C/fan oven 180°C.

2 Cut a pocket in each cod fillet and fill with a little of the soft
cheese. Press the fish together to enclose the filling and then
dip in the beaten egg.

3 Stir some seasoning and the parsley into the breadcrumbs
and then coat each piece of the fish with the breadcrumb
mixture. Lift on to a baking tray lined with non stick baking
parchment. Spray evenly with the cooking spray, turning the
fish over to ensure the bottom is sprayed.

4 Bake for 20 minutes, until the fish is cooked through.

Tip... Check for any small bones by running your fingers
over the surface of the cod, and remove them using small
tweezers.

Family fish pie

Serves 6
277 calories per serving
Takes 35 minutes to prepare, 20 minutes to cook

An easy fish pie that's great for a midweek supper. Serve with your favourite vegetables,
such as broccoli and carrots.

450 g (1 lb) floury potatoes, peeled and cut
   into chunks
450 g (1 lb) pumpkin or butternut squash,
   peeled, de-seeded and cut into chunks
600 ml (20 fl oz) skimmed milk
2 bay leaves
500 g (1 lb 2 oz) cod fillets
calorie controlled cooking spray
1 large onion, sliced
2 garlic cloves, crushed

4 celery sticks or a small fennel bulb,
   chopped finely
150 g (5½ oz) mushrooms, sliced
100 g (3½ oz) frozen sweetcorn or peas
2 tablespoons cornflour
a small bunch of fresh parsley, chopped
1 heaped teaspoon French mustard
100 g (3½ oz) half fat mature Cheddar cheese
salt and freshly ground black pepper

1 Bring a pan of water to the boil, add the potatoes and pumpkin or butternut squash and cook for
20 minutes, or until tender. Strain but reserve the cooking water. Mash the vegetables together and
season.

2 Meanwhile, in a large non stick frying pan, heat the milk with the bay leaves and fish fillets until
it comes to the boil. Simmer for 1 minute, or until the fish is almost cooked through. Remove the
fish to a plate, strain the milk into a small saucepan and reserve.

3 Rinse the frying pan and spray with the cooking spray. Fry the onion and garlic for 5 minutes,
until softened, adding 1–2 tablespoons of the reserved cooking water if necessary to prevent them
from sticking.

continues overleaf ▶

4 Add the celery or fennel and a few more tablespoons of the reserved cooking water and cook for a further 5 minutes. Add the mushrooms and cook on a high heat for 3 minutes, until the mushrooms start to give out their juices. Remove from the heat. This mixture needs to be dry, so drain off any juices.

5 Break up the fish, removing any skin and bones, and fold into the vegetables with the sweetcorn or peas. Transfer the whole mixture to a large ovenproof dish.

6 Preheat the oven to Gas Mark 6/200°C/fan oven 180°C. Take a couple of tablespoons of the reserved milk and mix with the cornflour. Stir this paste back into the rest of the milk and bring to the boil, stirring, until it thickens. Add the parsley, mustard and seasoning.

7 Pour the parsley sauce over the fish mixture and fold gently together. Top with the potato and squash mash. Scatter over the grated cheese and bake for 20 minutes, until the cheese is golden and bubbling.

Tip... To skin fish, lay the fish fillet skin side down and make a small cut at the tail end, through the flesh to the skin. Place the fish with the tail towards you, then put the blade of the knife under the flesh where it has been cut. Holding the skin firmly with your other hand slide the blade away from you, up to the head of the fish, then discard the skin.

Special egg fried rice

Serves 4
365 calories per serving
Takes 35 minutes
❄

calorie controlled cooking
   spray
1 onion, chopped
150 g (5½ oz) carrots, peeled
   and chopped finely
1 red pepper, de-seeded and
   chopped finely
225 g (8 oz) dried long grain
   rice
2 tablespoons soy sauce
½ teaspoon Chinese five spice
600 ml (20 fl oz) vegetable or
   chicken stock
100 g (3½ oz) lean ham, diced
100 g (3½ oz) cooked peeled
   prawns, defrosted if frozen
150 g (5½ oz) beansprouts
2 eggs

Egg fried rice no longer needs to be a weekend treat. This simple version is much healthier than a portion from a Chinese take-away, but just as delicious.

1 Heat a large, lidded, non stick saucepan and spray it with the cooking spray. Add the onion, carrots and pepper and stir-fry for 2 minutes. Stir in the rice, soy sauce, Chinese five spice and stock and bring to the boil. Reduce the heat, cover and simmer for 10 minutes.

2 Remove the lid, turn up the heat and add the ham, prawns and beansprouts.

3 Beat the eggs with 3 tablespoons of water. Push the rice to one side of the pan and spray some more cooking spray in the cleared space. Pour the eggs into the cleared space and cook until they set.

4 Break up the cooked egg with a spatula and incorporate it into the rice mixture. Spoon into four serving bowls and serve with extra soy sauce, if you like.

Variation... Use leftover chicken instead of the ham if you like. Simply shred the meat with two forks and add it to the rice in step 2.

Tuna, courgette and leek lasagne

Serves 4

400 calories per serving

Takes 40 minutes to prepare,
  35 minutes to cook

❄

**calorie controlled cooking
  spray**

1 onion, chopped

2 garlic cloves, crushed

1 leek, chopped finely

400 g can chopped tomatoes

2 tablespoons tomato purée

**2 courgettes, halved
  lengthways and sliced**

1 teaspoon dried oregano

**240 g can tuna in brine,
  drained and flaked**

**110 g (4 oz) no precook
  lasagne sheets**

**110g (4 oz) half fat mature
  Cheddar cheese, grated**

**salt and freshly ground black
  pepper**

For the white sauce

4 teaspoons low fat spread

25 g (1 oz) plain white flour

300 ml (10 fl oz) skimmed milk

1 teaspoon English mustard

*This recipe offers a wonderful alternative to traditional
lasagne.*

1 Preheat the oven to Gas Mark 5/190°C/fan oven 170°C.

2 Spray a lidded non stick saucepan with the cooking spray,
add the onion, garlic and leek and cook for 5 minutes, or until
softened. Stir in the tomatoes, tomato purée, courgettes and
oregano. Bring to the boil and then reduce the heat, cover and
simmer gently for 15 minutes.

3 Meanwhile, prepare the white sauce. Melt the low fat spread
in a small saucepan, stir in the flour and cook for 1 minute.
Gradually whisk in the milk and cook, whisking continuously,
until the sauce thickens. Remove the pan from the heat, stir in
the mustard and season well.

4 Mix the tuna into the tomato sauce and season. Spoon half
of the tomato mixture into a shallow ovenproof dish and top
with half the lasagne sheets. Spread half the white sauce over
and then sprinkle with half of the cheese. Repeat the layers in
the same order to use up the remaining ingredients, finishing
with a sprinkling of cheese.

5 Bake for 35 minutes, until bubbling and golden.

Paella

Serves 6
345 calories per serving
Takes 20 minutes to prepare, 45 minutes to cook ❄

The name 'paella' actually refers to the large flat cooking pan in which this famous Spanish fish recipe is cooked. It's one of the great dishes of the world.

a pinch of saffron strands
1.2 litres (2 pints) hot fish or chicken stock
calorie controlled cooking spray
2 garlic cloves, crushed
a bunch of spring onions, chopped finely
1 red pepper, de-seeded and chopped
350 g (12 oz) dried risotto rice
225 g (8 oz) squid rings
350 g (12 oz) cooked prawns in shells

450 g (1 lb) fresh mussels, prepared (see Tip on page 18)
2 tablespoons chopped fresh parsley
1 bay leaf
125 ml (4 fl oz) dry white wine
1 tablespoon lemon juice
50 g (1¾ oz) frozen petit pois or garden peas
salt and freshly ground black pepper
lemon wedges and chopped fresh parsley, to garnish

1 Add the saffron strands to the hot stock and let them infuse for 10–15 minutes.

2 Heat a wok or large frying pan and spray it with the cooking spray. Add the garlic, spring onions and pepper. Sauté them for about 5 minutes until softened.

3 Add the rice to the wok or frying pan and sauté for 1 minute. Pour in the saffron infused hot stock and bring to the boil. Reduce the heat and simmer for 10 minutes.

4 Add all the remaining ingredients, apart from the garnish, and stir well. Cook gently, uncovered, for about 20 minutes, stirring occasionally, until the liquid has been absorbed and the rice is tender. Add a little extra liquid if it has all been absorbed before the rice is cooked.

5 Discard the bay leaf and any mussels that have not opened during cooking. Season well and then serve, garnished with lemon wedges and parsley.

Variation... To make a chicken paella, replace the squid and mussels with 350 g (12 oz) chopped skinless cooked chicken breast 10 minutes before the end of the cooking time.

Spice is nice

Grilled cod with a Caribbean salsa

Serves 4
145 calories per serving
Takes 20 minutes

**4 x 150 g (5½ oz) cod steaks
  or fillets**
1 teaspoon vegetable oil

For the salsa
1 small red onion
1 green chilli, de-seeded
**1 red pepper, de-seeded and
  quartered**
a handful of fresh basil leaves
juice of 2 limes
**2 tomatoes, de-seeded and
  diced finely**
2 pineapple rings, diced finely
salt

*Liven up a plainly grilled cod steak with this feisty salsa.
The opposing flavours and textures are surprisingly good
together. This dish is delicious served with mashed sweet
potato and courgettes.*

1 To make the salsa, finely chop the onion and chilli in a food
processor, until they are almost like a purée, and then add the
red pepper and basil leaves. Take care to make sure that you
only process them lightly so that the red pepper is still a little
chunky.

2 Stir in the lime juice, tomatoes and pineapple and season
with salt. Cover and set aside.

3 Brush the cod steaks or fillets with a little oil. Cook under
a medium grill for 3–4 minutes on each side or until tender.
Spoon the salsa on to the grilled cod to serve.

Tip... Take great care when handling fresh chillies. Wash
your hands thoroughly immediately after handling or, better
still, wear disposable gloves. If you should accidentally
touch your eyes, bathe them with water.

Thai style mussels

Serves 2
372 calories per serving
Takes 20 minutes

calorie controlled cooking
  spray
1 onion, chopped
2 garlic cloves, chopped
1 tablespoon Thai red curry
  paste
175 ml (6 fl oz) hot fish or
  vegetable stock
75 ml (3 fl oz) dry white wine
juice of a lime
800 g (1 lb 11 oz) fresh
  mussels, prepared (see Tip
  on page 18)
2 tablespoons chopped fresh
  coriander

*Mussels are easier to prepare and cook than you might
think, so give this simple supper a try.*

1 Spray a large, lidded, non stick saucepan with the cooking
spray and fry the onion for 6 minutes until softened. Add the
garlic and cook for another minute.

2 Dissolve the Thai red curry paste in the hot stock and pour
it into the pan. Add the wine. Bring to the boil, reduce the heat
and simmer, half covered, for 2 minutes.

3 Stir in half of the lime juice, add the mussels, cover and
cook over a medium heat for 3 minutes, shaking the pan
occasionally.

4 Add the rest of the lime juice and half the coriander, stir
well and then cover and cook for a further 1–2 minutes or until
the mussels have opened. Discard any mussels that have not
opened.

5 Serve in large bowls, sprinkled with the remaining coriander.

Indian seafood noodles

Serves 4

420 calories per serving

Takes 5 minutes to prepare,
  25 minutes to cook

**calorie controlled cooking
  spray**

2 onions, chopped

2 garlic cloves, chopped

**400 g (14 oz) seafood
  selection, defrosted if frozen**

2 tablespoons curry paste

**150 ml (5 fl oz) fish or
  vegetable stock**

400 g can chopped tomatoes

250 g (9 oz) dried noodles

**25 g packet fresh coriander,
  chopped**

**250 g (9 oz) low fat natural
  yogurt**

**salt and freshly ground black
  pepper**

*This recipe borrows from the delicious creamy seafood
curries that you find in Southern India.*

1 Spray a large non stick frying pan or wok with the cooking
spray and put over a medium heat. Stir-fry the onions and
garlic for 4 minutes or until soft. Add the seafood, curry paste,
stock and tomatoes and simmer for 20 minutes.

2 Meanwhile, bring a pan of water to the boil, add the noodles
and cook according to the packet instructions.

3 Take the curry off the heat, check the seasoning and stir in
the coriander and yogurt. Serve with the plain noodles.

Tip... For a more authentic curry flavour it is best to use
whole spices like coriander seeds, cumin seeds, fennel
seeds and turmeric. Grind them up in a food processor or
in a mortar and pestle. Add a teaspoon of each spice to the
curry, instead of the curry paste.

Spiced salmon with pea purée

Serves 4
339 calories per serving
Takes 15 minutes

1 tablespoon medium curry
  powder
1 teaspoon cumin seeds
juice of ½ a lemon
4 x 125 g (4½ oz) skinless
  salmon fillets
calorie controlled cooking
  spray
400 g (14 oz) frozen peas
2 heaped tablespoons
  chopped fresh coriander
2 tablespoons half fat crème
  fraîche
2 tablespoons skimmed milk
freshly ground black pepper

*Fish is so quick to cook that it makes the perfect speedy
supper. Adding spices livens up the meal for no extra
effort.*

1 In a small bowl, mix the curry powder, cumin seeds and
lemon juice to a paste. Spread over both sides of the salmon
fillets and season with black pepper.

2 Heat a non stick frying pan until hot and spray with the
cooking spray. Add the salmon fillets and cook for 4 minutes
on each side over a medium heat until lightly caramelised
and just cooked through.

3 Meanwhile, bring a pan of water to the boil, add the peas
and cook for 2–3 minutes until tender. Drain and transfer to
a food processor with the coriander, crème fraîche and milk.
Whizz to a rough purée. Season with black pepper and serve
with the spiced salmon.

American shrimp

Serves 4
435 calories per serving
Takes 35 minutes

**800 g (1 lb 11 oz) potatoes,
peeled and cut into large
chunks**
**4 lean back bacon rashers, fat
and rind removed and cut
into thin strips**
450 g (1 lb) frozen sweetcorn
**400 g (14 oz) frozen, cooked,
peeled prawns**

For the seasoning
**2 tablespoons yellow mustard
seeds**
**½ tablespoon black
peppercorns**
**½ tablespoon dried chilli
flakes**
1 bay leaf
½ tablespoon coriander seeds
½ tablespoon ground ginger
1 tablespoon ground mace
1 tablespoon salt

*This is a distinctively spicy stew, popular in the southern
states of America.*

1 Bring 1.2 litres (2 pints) of water to the boil in a large pan.
Meanwhile, put all the seasoning ingredients except the
salt into a spice mill or pestle and mortar and grind to a fine
powder. Add the salt and blend very quickly.

2 Add all but 2 tablespoons of the seasoning mixture to
the boiling water, then add the potatoes and simmer for
15 minutes.

3 Add the bacon and sweetcorn to the pan and simmer for
5 minutes. Add the prawns and cook for 5 minutes without
boiling. Drain.

4 Serve piled on to plates with the reserved seasoning mix
sprinkled over the top.

Squid in spicy spinach sauce

Serves 4

335 calories per serving

Takes 10 minutes to prepare,
15 minutes to cook

**calorie controlled cooking
spray**

½ onion, chopped finely

2 garlic cloves, chopped finely

**1 cm (½ inch) fresh root
ginger, grated**

½ teaspoon ground cumin

½ teaspoon ground coriander

½ teaspoon turmeric

¼ teaspoon chilli powder

2 tomatoes, chopped

**200 g (7 oz) frozen spinach,
defrosted**

250 g (9 oz) dried egg noodles

**300 g (10½ oz) fresh squid, cut
into strips**

**salt and freshly ground black
pepper**

*An unusual but delicious way to serve squid, with lots of
lovely spices and a creamy spinach sauce.*

1 Heat a non stick frying pan and spray with the cooking spray.
Add the onion, garlic and ginger and stir-fry for 3–4 minutes.

2 Add the spices and stir well before adding the tomatoes and
spinach. Stir well again and pour in 200 ml (7 fl oz) of water.
Bring to a simmer and cook for 4–5 minutes.

3 Meanwhile, bring a pan of water to the boil, add the noodles
and cook according to the packet instructions. Drain well.

4 Add the squid to the frying pan and simmer for 4–5 minutes
until the squid is cooked. Check the seasoning and serve with
the noodles.

Spicy prawn cakes

Serves 4
136 calories per serving
Takes 20 minutes +
   30 minutes chilling

For the prawn cakes
200 g (7 oz) raw peeled tiger prawns, defrosted if frozen
200 g (7 oz) skinless white fish fillets (e.g. monkfish or coley), chopped roughly
1 tablespoon red Thai curry paste
1 tablespoon cornflour
4 spring onions, sliced finely
calorie controlled cooking spray

For the dipping sauce
juice of a lime
4 tablespoons sweet chilli sauce
1 heaped tablespoon chopped fresh coriander

Great for a dinner party starter or nibble, these yummy prawn cakes can be made ahead and simply reheated just before your guests arrive.

1 Place the prawns, white fish, curry paste and cornflour in a food processor and blend until quite finely chopped. Remove the mixture from the food processor and place in a bowl. Mix in the spring onions, cover and chill the mixture in the fridge for 30 minutes.

2 To make the dipping sauce, mix the lime juice, chilli sauce and coriander together in a small bowl. Set aside.

3 Using wet hands, carefully shape the prawn mixture into 12 small cakes. Spray a large non stick frying pan with the cooking spray and place on a medium-high heat. Add six prawn cakes and fry for 2 minutes on each side until browned and firm. Keep warm while you cook the remaining prawn cakes. Serve with the dipping sauce.

Tip... To reheat, spread out in a single layer on a non stick baking tray, cover with foil and heat through for 10 minutes in an oven preheated to Gas Mark 4/180°C/fan oven 160°C.

Chilli crab noodles

Serves 2
455 calories per serving
Takes 20 minutes

150 g (5½ oz) dried vermicelli
noodles

a kettleful of boiling water

2 teaspoons sunflower oil

1 small red pepper, de-seeded
and sliced thinly

100 g (3½ oz) baby corn,
halved

6 spring onions, sliced

200 g (7 oz) canned white crab
meat, drained

2 tablespoons sweet chilli
sauce

2 tablespoons tomato ketchup

1 tablespoon soy sauce

2 tablespoons chopped fresh
coriander, to serve (optional)

*When time is of the essence, create this tasty dish from
start to finish in less than 20 minutes.*

1 Place the noodles in a bowl and cover them with boiling
water. Leave them to stand for 5 minutes and then drain
thoroughly.

2 Meanwhile, heat the oil in a non stick pan or wok and stir-fry
the red pepper and baby corn for 2–3 minutes. Add the drained
noodles, spring onions, crab meat, sweet chilli sauce, tomato
ketchup and soy sauce and stir-fry for 2–3 minutes.

3 Scatter over the chopped fresh coriander, if using, and serve.

Tip... Vermicelli noodles can go very soggy if left standing
around for too long, so serve this dish immediately and
avoid over soaking the noodles – 5 minutes is plenty of
time as they are thinner than ordinary noodles.

Moroccan fish tagine

Serves 4

235 calories per serving

Takes 15 minutes to prepare,
  35 minutes to cook

❄

1 tablespoon olive oil

1 onion, sliced

150 g (5½ oz) carrots, peeled
  and sliced

225 g (8 oz) potatoes, peeled
  and cubed

2 celery sticks, sliced

100 g (3½ oz) mushrooms,
  sliced

½ teaspoon ground cinnamon

½ teaspoon paprika

½ teaspoon dried chilli flakes

1 teaspoon ground coriander

½ teaspoon cumin seeds

2 bay leaves

25 g (1 oz) sultanas

400 g can chopped tomatoes

2 tablespoons tomato purée

300 ml (10 fl oz) fish stock

350 g (12 oz) skinless cod
  fillet, cubed

salt and freshly ground black
  pepper

2 tablespoons chopped fresh
  coriander, to garnish

*A warmly spiced casserole, full of the flavours of the
mysterious East. For a really traditional meal, serve with
couscous.*

1 Heat the oil in a large, lidded, flameproof casserole dish with
2 tablespoons of water and add the onion, carrots, potatoes,
celery and mushrooms. Cook, stirring, for 2 minutes and then
stir in the spices, bay leaves and sultanas.

2 Add the chopped tomatoes, tomato purée and stock and
bring to the boil. Cover and simmer for 20 minutes, until the
vegetables are tender. Remove the lid, add the fish and cook for
a further 10 minutes, until the fish is cooked through. Remove
the bay leaves and season to taste.

3 Spoon into warmed serving bowls and scatter with the
coriander to serve.

Thai fish curry

Serves 4
225 calories per serving
Takes 25–30 minutes to prepare, 20–25 minutes to cook ❄

Miles of coastline surround Thailand, so it's no surprise that fish curries are so popular.

calorie controlled cooking spray
6 shallots or 1 large onion, sliced
1 garlic clove, sliced thinly
200 ml (7 fl oz) reduced fat coconut milk
425 ml (15 fl oz) vegetable stock
3–4 teaspoons Thai green curry paste
350 g (12 oz) butternut squash, peeled, de-seeded and cut into chunks
1 red pepper, de-seeded and cut into chunks
125 g (4½ oz) fine green beans, halved
2 tablespoons chopped fresh coriander

1 tablespoon fish sauce or light soy sauce
1 teaspoon ready-prepared ginger from a jar
1 teaspoon ready-prepared lemongrass from a jar
1 green chilli, de-seeded and sliced thinly (optional)
200 g (7 oz) skinless haddock fillet, cut into chunks
200 g (7 oz) cooked tiger prawns with tails, defrosted if frozen
salt and freshly ground black pepper
fresh coriander sprigs, to garnish

1 Heat a wok or large non stick frying pan and lightly spray it with the cooking spray. Add the shallots or onion and garlic and cook over a medium heat for about 4–5 minutes, until softened.

2 Add all the remaining ingredients, apart from the haddock, prawns and coriander. Bring to the boil. Reduce the heat and simmer gently for about 20–25 minutes, until the butternut squash is tender.

3 Add the fish to the pan and cook for 2–3 minutes. Add the prawns and cook for another 2–3 minutes. Check the seasoning.

4 Ladle the curry into four bowls and serve, garnished with fresh coriander sprigs.

Tip... Cook curries according to your own taste, so add a little curry paste at first if you're not sure how hot you want it to be. You can always add a little more as you go.

Cajun mackerel fillets with crispy sweet vegetables

Serves 2
485 calories per serving
Takes 20 minutes

2 x 175 g (6 oz) mackerel fillets, skin left on
½ teaspoon Cajun seasoning
2 shallots, quartered
1 small green or red pepper, de-seeded and cut into chunks
2 small carrots, scrubbed
2 small courgettes
1 tablespoon soy sauce
1 tablespoon light brown soft sugar
1 tablespoon rice vinegar or cider vinegar
1 tablespoon tomato ketchup

Oily fish, such as mackerel, trout and sardines, should be included on your shopping list every week. Here is a tasty, quick recipe to encourage the habit.

1 Heat a non stick frying pan. Sprinkle the skinless side of the mackerel with the Cajun seasoning. Place seasoned side down in the hot pan and cook for 2–3 minutes over a moderate heat. Turn the pieces over and cook for a further 2–3 minutes or until the fish flakes easily and is slightly charred.

2 Remove from the pan and keep warm. Add the shallots, pepper and 4 tablespoons of water to the pan. Cook for 3 minutes, shaking the pan frequently. Use a potato peeler to slice the carrots and courgettes into ribbons. Add to the pan together with the remaining ingredients and stir-fry for 2 minutes.

3 Serve the mackerel with the crunchy vegetables.

Tip... Rice wine vinegar is a slightly sweet and mildly acidic vinegar, popular in Asian cookery. Use it in vinaigrettes for a much lighter flavour.

Variation... Replace the mackerel with trout or salmon fillets. The richness of the oily fish works well with the sweet and sour vegetables.

Spicy grilled sardines

Serves 4

278 calories per serving

Takes 20 minutes

½ teaspoon paprika

1 teaspoon cumin seeds

4 garlic cloves, chopped roughly

1 tablespoon lemon juice

2 teaspoons olive oil

600 g (1 lb 5 oz) fresh sardines, cleaned, with bones left in

salt and freshly ground black pepper

mixed green leaf salad, to serve

These are particularly delicious cooked on a hot barbecue.

1 Preheat the grill to a high heat or ensure your barbecue is ready.

2 Put the paprika and cumin seeds in a pestle and grind them into a powder with the mortar. Add the garlic and crush well, then mix in the lemon juice and olive oil and season.

3 Place the sardines on a grill rack and brush the oil mixture over the sardines. Grill for 2–3 minutes. Turn the sardines over, brush again with the remaining oil mixture and cook for a further 2 minutes. When the flesh of the fish turns white they are cooked. Serve immediately with the salad.

Tip... To remove the main bones once cooked, open the fish out, skin side down, and gently pull up the central bone from the tail end.

Goan style salmon

Serves 4
336 calories per serving
Takes 21 minutes

1 red chilli, de-seeded and chopped

2.5 cm (1 inch) fresh root ginger, chopped

1 lemongrass stalk, outer leaves discarded, chopped finely

2 tablespoons Goan spice blend or korma curry powder

200 g (7 oz) low fat soft cheese

200 ml (7 fl oz) hot fish stock

4 x 150 g (5½ oz) skinless salmon fillets

2 teaspoons turmeric

calorie controlled cooking spray

This is a fantastic way to liven up salmon and the whole family will love it. Serve with 60 g (2 oz) dried brown rice per person, cooked according to the packet instructions, and steamed green beans.

1 To make the sauce, put the chilli, ginger and lemongrass into a food processor and whizz to a coarse paste. Add the spice blend or curry powder and soft cheese and whizz again. Gradually add the fish stock until everything is combined to create a sauce.

2 Coat the salmon fillets in the turmeric. Heat a wide, lidded, non stick pan and spray with the cooking spray. Cook the salmon fillets for 1 minute on each side until golden brown.

3 Pour over the sauce and bring to the boil. Cover and simmer for 10 minutes until the salmon is cooked and the sauce has thickened. Serve immediately.

Spicy prawn and spinach curry

Serves 4

250 calories per serving

Takes 5 minutes to prepare,
20 minutes to cook

½ teaspoon mustard seeds

½ teaspoon fennel seeds

calorie controlled cooking
spray

2.5 cm (1 inch) fresh root
ginger, grated

2 garlic cloves, diced finely

2 onions, chopped finely

1 teaspoon cumin seeds

1 teaspoon coriander seeds

½ teaspoon turmeric

1 small red or green chilli,
de-seeded and chopped
finely

100 ml (3½ fl oz) vegetable
stock

400 g can chopped tomatoes

450 g (1 lb) spinach, defrosted
if frozen

1 tablespoon soy sauce

450 g (1 lb) cooked peeled
prawns, defrosted if frozen

200 g (7 oz) half fat crème
fraîche

a bunch of fresh coriander,
chopped

Although this recipe has a lot of ingredients, it is really quick and easy to make. Serve with 60 g (2 oz) dried rice per person, cooked according to the packet instructions.

1 Grind the mustard seeds and fennel seeds in a spice grinder or crush using a pestle and mortar.

2 Spray a large, lidded, non stick frying pan or wok with the cooking spray and stir-fry the ginger, garlic, onions, spices, seeds and chilli with the stock until the stock has boiled away and the onions are soft.

3 Add the tomatoes, spinach and soy sauce and allow to simmer for 10 minutes, covered.

4 Add the prawns and stir through. Simmer for 3–4 minutes, remove from the heat, stir in the crème fraîche and coriander and serve.

Indonesian baked fish with chilli chutney

Serves 4

135 calories per serving

Takes 20 minutes to prepare,
  30 minutes to cook

✳

450 g (1 lb) skinless cod fillet,
  divided into 4 equal pieces

1 garlic clove, crushed

1 red chilli, de-seeded and
  sliced finely

2 tablespoons fish sauce

1 tablespoon demerara sugar

3 tablespoons chopped fresh
  coriander

finely grated zest and juice of
  a lime

For the chilli chutney

1 teaspoon sunflower oil

1 onion, sliced

1 red chilli, de-seeded and
  chopped finely

1 tablespoon rice wine vinegar

1 teaspoon demerara sugar

You can use any firm white fish in this spicy unusual dish.

1 To make the chutney, heat the oil in a lidded non stick pan and add the onion and chilli. Cover the pan and cook over a low heat for 10 minutes, stirring from time to time until the onions have softened. Add the vinegar and sugar and stir well. Cover and cook for a further 5 minutes.

2 Meanwhile, preheat the oven to Gas Mark 6/200°C/ fan oven 180°C. Rinse the fish fillets and pat dry with kitchen towel. Place skin side down in a non stick roasting tin.

3 Mix together the garlic, chilli, fish sauce, sugar, coriander and lime zest and juice and pour over the fish. Bake for 20 minutes or until the fish is cooked through. Serve the fish fillets topped with the chilli chutney.

Prawn laksa

Serves 4
295 calories per serving
Takes 30 minutes

125 g (4½ oz) dried rice noodles
a kettleful of boiling water
calorie controlled cooking spray
4 shallots, sliced
2 teaspoons ready-prepared lemongrass from a jar
2 teaspoons finely grated fresh root ginger
200 ml (7 fl oz) reduced fat coconut milk
200 ml (7 fl oz) vegetable stock
3–4 teaspoons Thai red curry paste
1 tablespoon fish sauce or light soy sauce
450 g (1 lb) large, cooked, peeled prawns, defrosted if frozen
1 tablespoon chopped fresh coriander, plus extra to garnish
1 red chilli, de-seeded and sliced finely, to garnish

This Malaysian soup is very popular throughout South East Asia.

1 Put the rice noodles into a bowl, cover them with boiling water and leave to soak for 4 minutes. Drain thoroughly.

2 Meanwhile, lightly spray a wok or large non stick frying pan with the cooking spray and sauté the shallots for about 3 minutes, until softened. Add the lemongrass, ginger, coconut milk, stock, curry paste and fish sauce or soy sauce. Heat until almost boiling.

3 Add the prawns to the wok or frying pan with the chopped coriander and cook gently for 2 minutes. Add the drained noodles and cook for a further 2 minutes, until they are heated through.

4 Serve the laksa in four warmed, shallow bowls, garnished with the chilli and coriander.

Speedy suppers

Grilled trout with Chinese vegetables

Serves 2
300 calories per serving
Takes 20 minutes

2 x 250 g (9 oz) whole trout
salt and freshly ground black pepper

For the stuffing
5 cm (2 inches) fresh root ginger, sliced into matchsticks
a bunch of spring onions, sliced into thin strips
100 g (3½ oz) mange tout, sliced into thin strips
2 carrots, peeled and sliced into thin strips
2 tablespoons soy sauce or tamari sauce
1 teaspoon sesame oil
a small bunch of fresh coriander, chopped

The fragrant stuffing for this grilled trout is also used as the accompanying salad.

1 Mix together all the stuffing ingredients in a bowl. Preheat the grill to medium high.

2 Season the trout, inside and out, and then place a small handful of the stuffing inside the cavity of each one. Grill for 5–10 minutes on each side, until cooked through and golden. Serve with the remaining stuffing as a salad.

Seared salmon with tangy avocado salsa

Serves 4
300 calories per serving
Takes 10 minutes

4 x 125 g (4½ oz) skinless
salmon fillets

calorie controlled cooking
spray

salt and freshly ground black
pepper

For the salsa

1 avocado, peeled, stoned and
diced

100 g (3½ oz) cherry
tomatoes, diced

grated zest and juice of
½ a lime

2 tablespoons fresh coriander,
chopped

*A quick 'summery' recipe that is just right served with
100 g (3½ oz) boiled new potatoes per person.*

1 Preheat a non stick frying pan. Lightly spray the salmon
fillets with the cooking spray and season. Cook for 2–3 minute
on each side, or until cooked to your liking.

2 While the salmon is cooking, mix the salsa ingredients
together and season. Serve the salsa spooned over the salmon

Tip... To prepare an avocado, cut in half and then run a
dessertspoon between the skin and the flesh to release it
easily in one piece. Remove the stone and dice or slice as
required.

Cod parcels with lemon and dill sauce

Serves 4
150 calories per serving
Takes 25 minutes

1 fennel bulb, sliced finely
4 x 150 g (5½ oz) cod steaks
grated zest and juice of a lemon
salt and freshly ground black pepper

For the sauce
calorie controlled cooking spray
2 shallots, sliced finely
grated zest and juice of a lemon
a small bunch of fresh dill, chopped finely
6 tablespoons virtually fat free plain fromage frais

This is a lovely, easy way to cook fish as the flavours are sealed in during cooking and each person opens their own parcel.

1 Preheat the oven to Gas Mark 6/200°C/fan oven 180°C. Cut four pieces of baking parchment, each about 30 cm (12 inches) square. Divide the fennel into four and pile in the centre of each piece of paper.

2 Lay a fish steak on top of each pile, season, scatter with the lemon zest and squeeze over the lemon juice. Lift up the opposite sides of the baking parchment, bring them together at the top and fold over a few times to seal. Fold over the open ends and tuck underneath the fish to make a sealed parcel. Place the parcels on a baking tray and bake for 15 minutes, until just cooked through.

3 Meanwhile, make the sauce. Spray a small saucepan with the cooking spray and stir-fry the shallots with a couple of tablespoons of water, until softened.

4 Squeeze in the lemon juice and allow to bubble, and then remove from the heat and stir in the lemon zest, dill and fromage frais. Season and serve with the fish.

Variation... The lemon and dill sauce also goes well with plain grilled fillets of fish or chicken breasts.

Prawn and ginger noodles

Serves 4
355 calories per serving
Takes 15 minutes

250 g (9 oz) dried fine egg noodles

calorie controlled cooking spray

a bunch of spring onions, sliced diagonally

2.5 cm (1 inch) fresh root ginger, cut into thin slivers

2 garlic cloves, sliced

1 red chilli, de-seeded and chopped finely (optional)

200 g (7 oz) cooked peeled prawns, defrosted if frozen

300 g (10½ oz) sugar snap peas or mange tout, sliced

2 teaspoons sesame oil

juice of a lemon

a bunch of fresh coriander, chopped, to garnish

Prawns with fresh ginger are a wonderful combination, conjuring up images of the East and sunny climes.

1 Bring a pan of water to the boil, add the noodles and cook according to the packet instructions. Drain, rinse with cold water and drain again.

2 Meanwhile, spray a wok or large non stick frying pan with the cooking spray and put on a high heat. Stir-fry the spring onions, ginger, garlic and chilli for 2 minutes.

3 Add the prawns, sugar snap peas or mange tout, sesame oil and lemon juice and stir-fry for a further 2 minutes. Add the noodles and toss together. Remove from the heat, sprinkle with the coriander and serve.

Herb-crusted plaice with tomatoes

Serves 2
291 calories per serving
Takes 15 minutes

calorie controlled cooking
  spray
2 medium slices white bread
finely grated zest and juice of
  ½ a lemon
25 g (1 oz) low fat spread,
  melted
1 tablespoon chopped fresh
  parsley
1 tablespoon chopped fresh
  lemon thyme
2 x 150 g (5½ oz) plaice fillets,
  skin left on
2 tomatoes, halved
freshly ground black pepper

*Serve with 150 g (5½ oz) cooked new potatoes per person
and some mange tout on the side.*

1 Preheat the grill to a medium heat and line the grill pan with foil. Spray with the cooking spray.

2 Roughly tear up the bread and then whizz to crumbs in a food processor. Mix with the lemon zest, half the lemon juice, the melted low fat spread, herbs and black pepper.

3 Arrange the plaice fillets and tomatoes side by side on the grill pan. Drizzle the rest of the lemon juice over the fish and then press the breadcrumb mixture firmly on to the plaice and the tomatoes.

4 Grill for 6–7 minutes until the topping is crisp and lightly browned, and the fish has cooked through. There is no need to turn the fish during cooking – it cooks through very easily. Serve immediately.

Sweet and sour prawns

Serves 4
239 calories per serving
Takes 20 minutes

227 g can pineapple pieces in natural juice
1 tablespoon cornflour
4 tablespoons cider vinegar
2 tablespoons soy sauce
1 tablespoon tomato purée
25 g (1 oz) light brown soft sugar
1 tablespoon vegetable oil
1 onion, sliced
1 red pepper, de-seeded and diced
1 green pepper, de-seeded and diced
2 large carrots, peeled and cut into matchsticks
300 g (10½ oz) raw peeled king prawns, defrosted if frozen
220 g can bamboo shoots, drained

Sweet and sour is a favourite Chinese take-away dish that is very simple to make at home. Serve with 60 g (2 oz) dried rice per person, cooked according to the packet instructions.

1 Drain the juice from the pineapple into a jug and whisk together with the cornflour, vinegar, soy sauce, tomato purée and sugar. Set the sauce aside.

2 Heat the oil in a wok or large non stick frying pan until smoking hot. Stir-fry the onion, peppers and carrots for 4 minutes and then stir in the prawns, bamboo shoots and pineapple pieces. Stir-fry for a further 2 minutes.

3 Pour in the sauce and 100 ml (3½ fl oz) of water. Bring to the boil and simmer, stirring until the sauce is thickened but clear. Serve immediately.

Variation... For sweet and sour chicken, add 350 g (12 oz) diced chicken breast in place of the prawns, but stir-fry for 4 minutes to cook the chicken through before adding the sauce.

Creamy crab linguine

Serves 2

20 calories per serving

Takes 5 minutes to prepare,
15 minutes to cook

5 g (2¾ oz) dried linguine or
tagliatelle

70 g can sweetcorn, drained

1-2 spring onions, chopped

3 g can dressed crab meat

tablespoons half fat crème
fraîche

few dashes of chilli sauce,
mild Chinese style or
Tabasco sauce

salt and freshly ground black
pepper

*Dressed crab is available in most supermarkets and it
works wonderfully in this simple and delicious seafood
sauce for pasta.*

1 Bring a pan of water to the boil, add the pasta and cook
according to the packet instructions. Drain, rinse in cold water
for a few moments and then return the pasta to the pan.

2 Heat the sweetcorn either in the microwave or in a small
saucepan. Mix it into the pasta along with the spring onions.

3 Beat the crab and crème fraîche together to make a smooth
mixture and add chilli sauce to taste. Stir the crab mixture into
the pasta. Reheat the pasta gently, season to taste and serve
immediately.

Pasta with cullen skink sauce

Serves 4
296 calories per serving
Takes 30 minutes

Cullen skink is a Scottish chowder, usually made with potatoes. This version uses pasta instead to turn the sauce into a delicious meal.

calorie controlled cooking spray
1 large leek, sliced thinly
1 small onion, chopped finely
300 ml (10 fl oz) skimmed milk
250 g (9 oz) smoked haddock fillet, skin left on
2 tablespoons plain white flour
2 tablespoons low fat crème fraîche
1 tablespoon finely chopped fresh parsley
160 g (5¾ oz) dried pasta shapes, such as penne
salt and freshly ground black pepper

1 Spray a non stick saucepan with the cooking spray, place over a medium heat and add the leek and onion. Cook for 10–12 minutes until softened, adding a little water if necessary to prevent them from sticking.

2 Meanwhile, put the milk in a large lidded frying pan, bring to the boil and then add the haddock. Return to the boil, remove from the heat, cover and leave to stand for 5 minutes. Remove the fish and reserve the milk. Skin the fish and break the flesh into flakes, removing and discarding any bones. Set aside.

3 When the leek and onion have softened, stir in the flour. Gradually add the milk from the cooked fish, stirring continuously. Bring gradually to a simmer, still stirring, and then simmer for 2 minutes. Stir in the crème fraîche and add the flaked fish, parsley and seasoning.

4 Meanwhile, bring a large pan of water to the boil and add the pasta. Cook for 8–9 minutes, or according to the packet instructions, until al dente. Drain well.

5 Add the pasta to the sauce and stir well to mix. Divide between four serving dishes and serve immediately.

Skate with butter and caper sauce

Serves 2
376 calories per serving
Takes 25 minutes

2 x 285 g (10 oz) skate wings,
  rinsed and patted dry
2 thick lemon slices
1 small onion, sliced
1 bay leaf
4 peppercorns
1½ tablespoons chopped fresh
  parsley, plus a few parsley
  stems
50 g (1¾ oz) half fat butter
1 tablespoon white wine
  vinegar
2 tablespoons capers in brine,
  rinsed well
2 medium slices crusty
  granary bread, to serve

*If you prefer to serve potatoes instead of bread, use
100 g (3½ oz) new potatoes per person.*

1 Put the skate into a shallow, large, lidded pan. Pour in
300 ml (10 fl oz) of water and add the lemon, onion, bay leaf,
peppercorns, parsley stems and half a tablespoon of the
chopped parsley. Bring to the boil, cover and poach for
15 minutes or until the fish comes away easily from the
bones.

2 Remove the fish with a fish slice, put on two warm plates
and discard the cooking liquid and flavourings. Keep the fish
warm while you make the sauce.

3 Wipe the pan clean with some kitchen towel and melt the
butter in the pan. Add the vinegar, remaining parsley and
capers. Mix well. Pour the sauce over the fish and serve with
the crusty bread.

Tips... The sauce also goes well with green beans and baby
carrots.

The cooking liquid from the fish makes excellent stock.
Simply pour it through a sieve after step 2, allow it to cool
and then store it in the fridge to use for another recipe for
up to 2 days.

Tuna polpettine

Serves 4
194 calories per serving
Takes 30 minutes
❄ (keep tuna balls and sauce
    separate)

225 g (8 oz) canned tuna in
    brine, drained and mashed
2 large spring onions, chopped
    very finely
150 g (5½ oz) fresh white
    breadcrumbs
1 egg, lightly beaten
calorie controlled cooking
    spray
salt and freshly ground black
    pepper

For the tomato sauce
1 garlic clove, crushed
400 g can chopped tomatoes
1 teaspoon dried oregano
1 tablespoon tomato purée
1 teaspoon tomato ketchup

These tuna meatballs are simple to make. Serve with
60 g (2 oz) dried pasta per person, cooked according to
the packet instructions.

1 Place the tuna, spring onions, breadcrumbs and egg in a
mixing bowl. Season and stir until well combined. With wet
hands, form the mixture into 16 balls, each about the size of
a walnut.

2 Spray a non stick frying pan with the cooking spray. Place
eight tuna balls in the pan and spray again. Cook, turning
occasionally, for about 6 minutes until golden. Remove and
keep warm. Repeat with the remaining tuna balls.

3 Meanwhile, make the tomato sauce. Spray a non stick
saucepan with the cooking spray and fry the garlic for
1 minute. Add the tomatoes, oregano, tomato purée, tomato
ketchup and 4 tablespoons of water. Bring to the boil, reduce
the heat and simmer for 10 minutes until thickened. Serve with
the tuna balls.

Trout with red pepper sauce

Serves 4
230 calories per serving
Takes 25 minutes

2 red peppers, de-seeded and
   halved
4 garlic cloves, unpeeled
1 tablespoon balsamic vinegar
calorie controlled cooking
   spray
4 x 150 g (5½ oz) trout fillets,
   skin left on
salt and freshly ground black
   pepper

*A delicious, bright red sauce perfectly complements the
strong trout flavour.*

1 Preheat the grill to hot and put the peppers, skin side up,
on the grill pan with the garlic cloves. Grill for 10 minutes until
blistered and blackened all over. Transfer into a plastic bag,
wrap up and leave to cool and 'sweat'.

2 When cool enough to handle, remove the skin from the
peppers and the garlic and place in a food processor with the
vinegar and seasoning. Blend to a purée.

3 Cover the grill pan with a piece of foil and spray with the
cooking spray. Place the trout fillets on the foil, skin side
up, and spread with some of the red pepper paste. Grill for
4–5 minutes until cooked through and the skin is crispy. Serve
with more of the sauce.

Tip... The purée is also good as a sauce for grilled meats,
especially chicken, and for baked potatoes.

Quick fish pie

Serves 4
378 calories per serving
Takes 30 minutes
❄ (before cooking in step 3)

half a kettleful of boiling water
150 g (5½ oz) broccoli, cut
  into small florets
30 g (1¼ oz) low fat spread
30 g (1¼ oz) plain white flour
400 ml (14 fl oz) skimmed milk
1 teaspoon Dijon mustard
250 g (9 oz) skinless salmon
  fillets, cubed
225 g (8 oz) skinless cod loin,
  cubed
100 g (3½ oz) shortcrust
  pastry, chilled
salt and freshly ground black
  pepper

*Serve with 100 g (3½ oz) cooked new potatoes per person
and green beans.*

1 Preheat the oven to Gas Mark 6/200°C/fan oven 180°C. Put
the boiling water in a saucepan and bring back to the boil. Add
the broccoli and cook for 2 minutes. Drain and set aside.

2 Melt the low fat spread in the saucepan that had the
broccoli. Add the flour and cook for 1 minute, stirring. Over
a low heat, gradually add the skimmed milk and whisk
continuously until smooth. Increase the heat and bring to the
boil, stirring until thickened.

3 Stir the broccoli, mustard, salmon and cod into the sauce.
Season. Spoon into four 300 ml (10 fl oz) ovenproof dishes or
a 1.2 litre (2 pint) dish. Grate the chilled pastry over the top
(it is very easy to grate when cold) and bake in the oven for
15 minutes until the pastry is golden and cooked.

Variation... You can use any type of white fish you like.
Pollock works really well and is a good sustainable food
source.

Asian tuna parcels

Serves 4
200 calories per serving
Takes 20 minutes

6 spring onions, sliced
2 garlic cloves, sliced thinly
5 cm (2 inches) fresh root ginger, cut into matchsticks
4 heads pak choi
4 x 150 g (5½ oz) fresh tuna steaks
4 tablespoons dark soy sauce

The aromatic flavourings of ginger, garlic and spring onions release a wonderful scent when the parcel is opened. Serve with 60 g (2 oz) dried brown rice per person cooked according to the packet instructions.

1 Preheat the oven to Gas Mark 6/200°C/fan oven 180°C.

2 Line a large roasting tin with a sheet of foil, big enough to double back over the roasting tin. Scatter half the spring onions, garlic and ginger over the base of the lined tin.

3 Cut each head of pak choi into quarters through the root and add to the roasting tin. Place the tuna steaks on top of the pak choi and scatter with the rest of the spring onions, garlic and ginger. Drizzle the soy sauce all over and then crimp the edges of the foil tightly to make a large parcel.

4 Bake in the oven for 12 minutes. Carefully undo the foil and serve the tuna on the bed of pak choi.

Prawn and mushroom pilaff

Serves 4
320 calories per serving
Takes 30 minutes
❄

225 g (8 oz) dried mixed wild
and white rice
15 g (½ oz) low fat spread
350 g (12 oz) chestnut
mushrooms, sliced
1 garlic clove, crushed
finely grated zest and juice of
an orange
1 tablespoon chopped fresh
tarragon
225 g (8 oz) raw peeled tiger
prawns, defrosted if frozen
salt and freshly ground black
pepper

A pilaff is a rice based dish. This one includes a filling mixture of prawns and mushrooms and a hint of citrus.

1 Bring a pan of water to the boil, add the rice and cook for about 25 minutes, or according to the packet instructions. Drain well.

2 Melt the low fat spread in a non stick frying pan. Add the mushrooms and garlic and stir-fry until the mushrooms are soft.

3 Add the orange zest and juice, tarragon and seasoning and allow the sauce to bubble for 2 minutes.

4 Mix in the cooked rice and prawns and cook, stirring, for a further 5 minutes, or until the prawns turn pink.

Filo fish bakes

Serves 4

288 calories per serving

Takes 10 minutes to prepare,
10 minutes to cook

**4 x 175 g (6 oz) skinless thick
cod fillets**

**small bunch of fresh dill,
chopped finely**

**100 g (3½ oz) low fat soft
cheese**

**200 g (7 oz) cooked peeled
prawns, defrosted if frozen**

**4 x 15 g (½ oz) filo pastry
sheets, measuring
30 x 40 cm (12 x 16 inches)**

**calorie controlled cooking
spray**

**25 g (1 oz) Parmesan cheese,
grated finely**

**salt and freshly ground black
pepper**

*Serve with 150 g (5½ oz) baked sweet potatoes per person,
and a winter salad of cooked beetroot with chopped dill,
a tablespoon of low fat natural yogurt and seasoning as a
dressing.*

1 Preheat the oven to Gas Mark 6/200°C/fan oven 180°C. Put
the fish on a non stick baking tray and season.

2 In a small bowl, mix together the dill and soft cheese and
then gently fold in the prawns. Season and pile evenly over
each fillet.

3 Spray each filo sheet with the cooking spray and then
scrunch each sheet up a little and arrange over the top of
a fillet.

4 Scatter with the Parmesan and bake for 10 minutes or until
the fish and prawns are cooked through and the pastry is crisp
and golden.

Prawns with chick peas and coriander

Serves 2
365 calories per serving
Takes 25 minutes

2 teaspoons olive oil

1 onion, halved and sliced thinly

1–2 garlic cloves, chopped, or 1–2 teaspoons garlic purée

1 small red chilli, de-seeded and chopped, or 1 teaspoon fresh chilli paste

400 g can chopped tomatoes with herbs

4 tablespoons dry white wine

2 teaspoons light soy sauce

2 teaspoons tomato purée

400 g can chick peas, drained and rinsed

175 g (6 oz) cooked peeled prawns, defrosted if frozen

4 tablespoons chopped fresh coriander

salt and freshly ground black pepper

This spicy seafood dish is perfect for a quick supper.

1 Heat the oil in a lidded non stick pan and cook the onion for 5 minutes until softened and lightly coloured. Add the garlic and chilli and cook for a further minute.

2 Add the tomatoes, wine, soy sauce and tomato purée. Simmer, covered, for 5 minutes.

3 Stir in the chick peas and prawns. Heat through for 3–4 minutes and then season to taste. Stir in the coriander. Cover and remove the pan from the heat. Leave to stand for 5 minutes to allow the coriander flavour to infuse.

Tip... If you don't want to cook with alcohol, omit the oil and wine, add an extra 200 g (7 oz) canned chopped tomatoes and cook all the ingredients in steps 1 and 2 together for 10 minutes, or until the onions are soft. Then proceed to step 3. This will add 5 minutes to the cooking time.

Variation... Replace the prawns with a 175 g (6 oz) cod fillet, cut into chunks. Add in step 3 and cook for 5 minutes.

Smoked mackerel pesto penne

Serves 4
295 calories per serving
Takes 20 minutes

150 g (5½ oz) dried penne
a kettleful of boiling water
150 g (5½ oz) broccoli,
  chopped into florets
12 cherry tomatoes, halved
140 g (5 oz) smoked mackerel
  fillets, skinned and flaked
3 tablespoons reduced fat
  pesto

Quick and easy, this is full of flavour and perfect for a midweek meal.

1 Bring a large pan of water to the boil, add the pasta and cook according to the packet instructions until al dente. Drain and rinse with boiling water.

2 Meanwhile, bring a second pan of water to the boil and steam or boil the broccoli for 3–5 minutes until just tender. Drain if necessary.

3 Stir all the remaining ingredients into the pasta with the broccoli and warm through over a low heat for 2–3 minutes until hot.

Baked cod with anchovies and garlic

Serves 4
280 calories per serving
Takes 35 minutes

4 x 175 g (6 oz) cod loins
50 g (1¾ oz) anchovies, drained
1 garlic clove, crushed
2 tablespoons tomato purée
450 g (1 lb) baby new potatoes, scrubbed
25 g (1 oz) low fat spread
1 tablespoon finely chopped fresh chives
freshly ground black pepper

Cod loins are widely available from supermarkets. They are the best part of the fillet, which has been skinned and trimmed into a neat, rounded piece of fish.

1 Preheat the oven to Gas Mark 5/190°C/fan oven 170°C. Place the cod loins on a non stick baking tray.

2 Pat the anchovies with kitchen towel to remove any excess oil. In a small bowl, mash the anchovies with the garlic and tomato purée to make a thick paste. Spread the anchovy paste over each cod loin. Bake the cod in the oven for 20 minutes.

3 Meanwhile, bring a pan of water to the boil, add the potatoes and cook for 15 minutes, until tender. Drain and, using a potato masher, break up the potatoes by lightly crushing them. Mix in the low fat spread and chives and season with plenty of black pepper.

4 Divide the crushed potatoes between four warmed serving plates and top each with a cod loin.

Simply special

Marinated prawns in lettuce boats

Makes 12 party bites
24 calories per serving
Takes 10 minutes +
marinating

100 g (3½ oz) virtually fat free
plain fromage frais
1 small garlic clove, crushed
1 teaspoon grated fresh root
ginger
grated zest and juice of ½ a
lemon
2 tablespoons chopped fresh
parsley
2 tablespoons chopped fresh
basil
300 g (10½ oz) cooked peeled
tiger prawns, defrosted if
frozen
2 Little Gem lettuces
salt and freshly ground black
pepper

The simplest summer buffet dish is quick and easy – the prawns just need time to marinate.

1 Stir the fromage frais together with the garlic, ginger and lemon zest and juice, mix in the herbs and season to taste. Stir the prawns into the mixture and set aside to marinate for 10–30 minutes.

2 Separate the lettuce leaves and arrange on a serving plate. Spoon a couple of prawns and a little of the marinade on to each lettuce leaf.

Smoked salmon tarts

Serves 6

141 calories per serving

Takes 5 minutes to prepare +
5 minutes standing,
25 minutes to cook

3 eggs

**150 g (5½ oz) low fat soft
cheese**

**1 tablespoon snipped fresh
chives**

**1½ tablespoons finely
chopped fresh dill**

grated zest of a large lemon

**300 g (10½ oz) thin smoked
salmon slices, cut into strips**

freshly ground black pepper

**50 g (1¾ oz) wild rocket, to
garnish**

*These pastry-free tarts are delicious hot or cold. They will
last in the fridge for up to 3 days and also make the perfect
starter for entertaining.*

1 Preheat the oven to Gas Mark 4/180°C/fan oven 160°C and
line a six hole muffin tin with muffin paper cases. To make
the filling, whisk together the eggs and soft cheese in a jug
until smooth. Stir in the chives, dill and lemon zest and season
generously with black pepper. Set aside.

2 Line each muffin case with strips of smoked salmon,
ensuring there are no gaps (it doesn't matter if the salmon
sticks up above the muffin cases). Pour in the filling and bake
in the oven for 20–25 minutes until set and golden.

3 Leave to stand for 5 minutes, then remove from the paper
cases and serve topped with a little wild rocket.

Prawn cocktail

Serves 4
120 calories per serving
Takes 10 minutes

6 tablespoons low fat natural yogurt
2 tablespoons tomato ketchup
1 tablespoon tartare sauce
350 g (12 oz) cooked peeled prawns, defrosted if frozen
1 bag herb salad leaves
1–2 teaspoons seasoned rice vinegar dressing or white wine vinegar
freshly ground black pepper

To garnish
1 tablespoon chopped fresh parsley (optional)
1 lime or lemon, sliced into wedges

Year in, year out, prawn cocktail ranks as one of our all-time favourite starters – probably because it tastes so good.

1 In a medium bowl, mix together the yogurt, tomato ketchup and tartare sauce. Add the prawns and stir gently to coat. Season with black pepper.

2 Toss the salad leaves in the seasoned vinegar dressing or white wine vinegar and then arrange on serving plates. Alternatively, shred the leaves and divide them between four attractive glasses.

3 Top the salad leaves with the prawn mixture. Garnish with the parsley, if using, and lime or lemon wedges and serve.

Tip... You can buy seasoned rice vinegar dressing from most supermarkets and delicatessens. It adds flavour and piquancy to salad leaves, so it's well worth looking out for.

Variation... For a spicier version, stir ½ teaspoon of de-seeded finely chopped green chilli and a tablespoon of chopped fresh coriander into the prawn mixture, omitting the parsley.

Asparagus stuffed plaice

Serves 2

370 calories per serving

Takes 20 minutes to prepare,
30 minutes to cook

**2 x 150 g (5½ oz) skinless
plaice fillets, cut in half
lengthways**

150 g (5½ oz) asparagus tips

**300 ml (10 fl oz) semi
skimmed milk**

**1 teaspoon wholegrain
mustard**

2 teaspoons low fat spread

1 tablespoon plain white flour

**40 g (1½ oz) grated Parmesan
cheese**

**salt and freshly ground black
pepper**

*These stuffed plaice are very light but have a delicious
rich, creamy sauce. They make an impressive and
attractive meal to serve to family and friends.*

1 Preheat the oven to Gas Mark 6/200°C/fan oven 180°C.

2 Lay the fillets on a board. Divide the asparagus tips between
the fillets and place them at the end of each fish. Gently roll up
the fillets, keeping the asparagus tips inside. Place the rolls in
an ovenproof baking dish.

3 Mix together the milk and mustard and pour over the rolls.
Season and place them in the oven for 30 minutes.

4 Remove the dish from the oven and pour off the milk,
reserving 150 ml (5 fl oz). Melt the low fat spread in a small
saucepan and mix in the flour. Pour the reserved milk into the
pan and bring to a simmer, stirring constantly until it starts to
thicken. Preheat the grill to high.

5 Pour the white sauce over the rolls and sprinkle over the
grated Parmesan. Grill the fish for 5–6 minutes or until golden.
Serve immediately.

Variation... For a real treat, stuff the plaice fillets with
100 g (3½ oz) prawns instead of the asparagus – cooking
for slightly less time.

Horseradish-crusted cod

Serves 4

0 calories per serving

Takes 30 minutes to prepare,
20 minutes to cook

200 g (7 oz) dried Puy lentils

**bunch of fresh parsley,
2 sprigs left whole and the
rest chopped finely**

**calorie controlled cooking
spray**

**4 x 125 g (4½ oz) skinless cod
fillets**

**1 tablespoon horseradish
sauce**

**tablespoons fresh white
breadcrumbs**

**tablespoons half fat crème
fraîche**

**salt and freshly ground black
pepper**

*These cod fillets are roasted with a horseradish crust and
served on a bed of creamy green lentils with herbs.*

1 Place the lentils in a pan and cover with water so it
comes about 5 cm (2 inches) above the top of the lentils.
Add the 2 whole parsley sprigs and bring to the boil. Simmer
for 20–30 minutes or until just tender.

2 Meanwhile, preheat the oven to Gas Mark 6/200°C/
fan oven 180°C and spray a non stick baking tray with the
cooking spray. Season both sides of the cod fillets and then
spread horseradish sauce thickly over the top of each.

3 Put the breadcrumbs on a plate and press the horseradish
side of each fillet down into the breadcrumbs so that they
stick. Place on the baking tray and bake for 20 minutes or
until the fish is cooked through.

4 When the lentils are cooked, drain and mix with most of
the chopped parsley and the crème fraîche, seasoning well.
Serve as a bed for the fish with the rest of the chopped parsley
scattered over the top.

Fish stew with saffron

Serves 6

125 calories per serving

Takes 15 minutes to prepare,
12 minutes to cook

**calorie controlled cooking
spray**
3 shallots, chopped
1 leek, sliced
2 carrots, peeled and diced
2 celery sticks, diced
400 g can chopped tomatoes
a pinch of saffron strands
600 ml (20 fl oz) hot fish stock
**400 g (14 oz) skinless cod
fillet, cut into bite size
pieces**
**200 g (7 oz) raw peeled
prawns, defrosted if frozen**
**a bunch of fresh parsley,
chopped**
**salt and freshly ground black
pepper**

*A wholesome, tasty fish dish. Serve with a 50 g (1¾ oz)
crusty brown roll per person to soak up the juices.*

1 Spray a large non stick pan with the cooking spray and add
the shallots, leek, carrots and celery. Stir-fry for 3–4 minutes
until starting to soften. Add the tomatoes and cook for another
2–3 minutes.

2 Meanwhile, add the saffron strands to the hot fish stock
and leave to infuse for 2 minutes.

3 Pour the saffron infused stock into the pan and add the
cod and prawns. Season and bring to a simmer. Simmer for
4–5 minutes until the prawns turn pink and the cod turns
white. Check the seasoning, stir in the chopped parsley and
serve.

Plaice rolls with a minty pea purée

Serves 4
160 calories per serving
Takes 25 minutes

225 g (8 oz) frozen peas
10–12 fresh mint leaves
4 tablespoons low fat natural
  yogurt
8 plaice fillets (about
  550 g/1 lb 3 oz in total)
a kettleful of boiling water
2 tablespoons lemon juice
2 teaspoons mint jelly
salt and freshly ground black
  pepper

*This is delicious with 150 g (5½ oz) cooked new potatoes
per person and steamed carrots.*

1 Bring a small pan of water to the boil, add the peas and
cook for 2–3 minutes until tender. Drain and refresh under cold
running water. Using a hand blender, whizz to a coarse purée
together with the mint and 2 tablespoons of the yogurt. Season
to taste.

2 Divide the purée between the fillets, roll up and arrange on
their ends in a frying pan. (The rolls need to fit snugly.) Pour
in just enough boiling water to cover the base of the pan and
then add the lemon juice. Cover tightly with foil and poach for
10 minutes, or until the fish turns opaque.

3 Transfer the fish to warm plates and reduce the liquid in the
pan to 4 tablespoons. Whisk in the mint jelly and remaining
yogurt, season to taste and drizzle over the plaice rolls.

Tip... Replace the mint jelly with mint sauce, if you prefer.

Mexican swordfish with spicy salsa

Serves 2

255 calories per serving

Takes 25 minutes + 1 hour
 marinating

**grated zest and juice of
 2 limes**

**a small bunch of fresh
 coriander, chopped**

**2 x 150 g (5½ oz) swordfish
 steaks**

**salt and freshly ground black
 pepper**

For the salsa

**1 mango, peeled, stoned and
 diced**

1 teaspoon chilli paste

**1 small red onion, chopped
 finely**

**3 tomatoes, quartered,
 de-seeded and chopped**

*This dish is delicious accompanied by a 225 g (8 oz) pota
per person, baked in its skin.*

1 Mix the lime zest, lime juice and half the coriander togethe
in a shallow dish, add the swordfish steaks and set aside to
marinate for 1 hour.

2 Meanwhile, mix together all the salsa ingredients with the
remaining coriander in a serving bowl.

3 Season the swordfish steaks. Cook them under a hot grill
or on a hot griddle for 4–5 minutes on each side, until just
cooked through and golden on the outside. Serve the fish w
the salsa.

Tip... This dish is great cooked on the barbecue.

Variation... For a change, try marlin, shark or tuna steaks.

Seafood provençale

Serves 4
425 calories per serving
Takes 15 minutes to prepare, 30–35 minutes to cook ❄

You'll love the robust flavours of this soupy fish stew. It will transport your tastebuds to the South of France.

1 tablespoon olive oil
1 large onion, sliced
1 large courgette, sliced
1 fennel bulb or 3 celery sticks, chopped
2 garlic cloves, crushed
1 aubergine, chopped
50 ml (2 fl oz) dry white wine
2 x 400 g cans chopped tomatoes
2 teaspoons dried herbes de Provence or mixed herbs

150 ml (5 fl oz) vegetable stock
450 g (1 lb) skinless cod fillet, cut into chunks
175 g (6 oz) large, cooked, peeled prawns, defrosted if frozen
1 tablespoon cornflour
salt and freshly ground black pepper
2 tablespoons chopped fresh parsley, to garnish
4 x 60 g (2 oz) slices French bread, to serve

1 Heat the oil in a large non stick saucepan and add the onion, courgette, fennel or celery, garlic and aubergine. Sauté for 4–5 minutes, until softened.

2 Pour in the wine and let it bubble up for a few moments. Add the tomatoes, dried herbs and stock and bring to the boil. Reduce the heat and simmer for 20 minutes, until the vegetables are tender.

3 Add the fish to the pan and cook for 3–4 minutes. Mix in the prawns and cook for another 2 minutes. Blend the cornflour to a paste with 2–3 tablespoons of cold water and add it to the pan, stirring gently. Cook for another 2 minutes, until the liquid is slightly thickened. Season to taste.

4 Ladle into four warmed soup plates or bowls and garnish with the parsley. Serve each with a slice of crusty French bread.

addock stuffed with mushrooms

rves 4
0 calories per serving
kes 10 minutes to prepare,
30 minutes to cook

- easpoon sunflower oil
- 5 g (8 oz) open cap
  mushrooms, chopped finely
- garlic clove, crushed
- ablespoon soy sauce
- easpoon dried parsley
- easpoon dried tarragon
- x 350 g (12 oz) skinless
  addock fillets
- g (1¾ oz) thinly sliced
  ancetta, prosciutto or
  arma ham
- lt and freshly ground black
  epper

This can be a real dinner party centrepiece. Prepare it ahead of time so all you have to do is pop it in the oven half an hour before you're ready to eat.

1 Heat the sunflower oil in a lidded non stick pan and add the mushrooms, garlic and soy sauce. Cover and cook over a low heat for 5 minutes, until softened. Stir in the parsley and tarragon and season.

2 Preheat the oven to Gas Mark 6/200°C/fan oven 180°C. Line a roasting tin with non stick baking parchment.

3 Lift the fish on to a clean board and use small tweezers to remove any bones. Top one piece with the cooked mushroom mixture and then cover with the other piece of fish to sandwich together.

4 Wrap the pancetta, prosciutto or Parma ham slices around the fish to help enclose the filling, lift it into the roasting tin and then cook for 30 minutes. Allow to stand for 5 minutes before slicing thickly to serve.

Lemon peppered tuna with courgettes

Serves 2
159 calories per serving
Takes 20 minutes

2 courgettes, cut into 3 mm
(⅛ inch) slices lengthways
calorie controlled cooking
spray
½ a lemon
½ red chilli, de-seeded and
diced
½ teaspoon crushed
peppercorns
2 x 100 g (3½ oz) tuna steaks

A simple but stunning recipe for when you want to treat someone special. Serve with 150 g (5½ oz) cooked new potatoes per person.

1 Preheat a griddle pan or the grill to a medium-high heat. Spray the courgette slices with the cooking spray and cook or grill for about 2 minutes on each side until browned and tender. Transfer to a plate and keep warm.

2 Meanwhile, finely grate the zest from the lemon and then cut the lemon half into two wedges. Mix the zest with the chilli and crushed peppercorns. Spray the tuna steaks with the cooking spray and coat with the lemon pepper mixture, pressing on well.

3 Cook or grill the tuna steaks and lemon wedges for 2–3 minutes on each side, depending on the thickness of the tuna, until the fish is just cooked through. Serve with the courgette ribbons, with the cooked lemon wedges to squeeze over.

Marinated trout fillets with apricot couscous

Serves 2

340 calories per serving

Takes 25 minutes + marinating

150 g (5½ oz) low fat natural yogurt

2 cm (¾ inch) fresh root ginger, grated finely

2 garlic cloves, crushed

1 small red chilli, de-seeded and chopped finely

400 g (14 oz) whole trout, filleted

50 g (1¾ oz) dried couscous

100 ml (3½ fl oz) boiling water

25 g (1 oz) dried apricots, chopped finely

a small bunch of fresh parsley, chopped finely

grated zest and juice of a lemon

salt and freshly ground black pepper

200 g (7 oz) cherry tomatoes, halved, to serve

A side salad of watercress or rocket with ripe tomatoes, a squeeze of lemon juice and seasoning makes a wonderful accompaniment.

1 Mix together the yogurt, ginger, garlic, chilli and seasoning and rub it over both sides of the trout fillets. Chill and leave to marinate for at least 30 minutes, but up to 2 hours.

2 Preheat the grill to medium high. Cook the fish under the hot grill for 4–5 minutes on each side, until golden and cooked through.

3 Meanwhile, put the couscous in a bowl and pour over the boiling water. Cover with a plate or other lid so that it will steam for 5 minutes.

4 Break up the steamed couscous with a fork and stir through the apricots, parsley, lemon zest, lemon juice and seasoning. Serve the trout on a bed of couscous with the tomatoes on the side.

Tip... The simple marinade used in this recipe can also be rubbed on lamb before grilling or used as a dip for crudités or roast vegetables.

Salmon and potato tart

Serves 4
335 calories per serving
Takes 40 minutes

300 g (10½ oz) waxy potatoes such as Charlotte, peeled and cut into 5 mm (¼ inch) slices

100 g (3½ oz) asparagus tips

8 x 15 g (½ oz) filo pastry sheets, measuring 30 x 40 cm (12 x 16 inches)

calorie controlled cooking spray

2 tablespoons hot horseradish sauce

125 ml (4 fl oz) soured cream

250 g (9 oz) skinless salmon fillets, cut into 1 cm (¼ inch) thick slices

salt and freshly ground black pepper

This filling tart is delicious hot or cold. Serve with a generous salad, drizzled with 1 tablespoon of light salad cream and 1 tablespoon of reduced fat coleslaw per person.

1 Preheat the oven to Gas Mark 6/200°C/fan oven 180°C. P• the potato slices in a large saucepan and cover with water. Bring to the boil and simmer for 5 minutes. Add the asparagu for the last minute and simmer. Drain, rinse in cold water and dry between sheets of kitchen towel.

2 Meanwhile, lay a sheet of filo pastry on a non stick baking tray and spray with the cooking spray. Take another filo sheet and lay it next to the other sheet to make a rectangle measuring 30 x 25 cm (12 x 10 inches). Spray again and repeat the layering until all the sheets are used.

3 Arrange the potato slices in a single layer, overlapping eac other slightly on top of the filo rectangle, leaving a 2½ cm (1 inch) border all the way around. Spray the exposed filo pastry with the cooking spray and fold the pastry over the potato slightly to make a case. Bake in the oven for 10 minut•

4 Meanwhile, in a bowl, mix together the horseradish sauce and soured cream. Remove the tart from the oven and sprea• the horseradish cream over the potato slices. Top with the salmon slices and asparagus tips and bake in the oven for 5–10 minutes until cooked. Cut into wedges and serve.

Ⓥ **Variation...** For a vegetarian option, replace the salmon with another 100 g (3½ oz) asparagus tips.

Parmesan lemon sole

Serves 4

170 calories per serving

Takes 20 minutes to prepare,
15 minutes to cook

❄

4 x 100 g (3½ oz) skinless
lemon sole fillets

2 tablespoons plain white
flour

50 g (1¾ oz) fresh white
breadcrumbs

25 g (1 oz) Parmesan cheese,
grated

1 egg, beaten

calorie controlled cooking
spray

salt and freshly ground black
pepper

*Lemon sole is a delicate fish with a soft texture. When yo
skin each fillet, you'll probably find that you end up with
two small fillets – this is fine. Serve this dish with freshly
cooked vegetables such as fine green beans and oven
roasted cherry tomatoes.*

1 Preheat the oven to Gas Mark 5/190°C/fan oven 170°C.

2 Rinse the sole fillets and pat them dry with kitchen towel.
Mix the flour with a little seasoning and dust this lightly over
each fillet.

3 Combine the breadcrumbs and Parmesan cheese in a
shallow dish. Dip each floured fillet in the beaten egg and the
into the breadcrumb mixture.

4 Spray the coated fillets with the cooking spray and lay ther
on a non stick baking tray. Bake for 15 minutes until the fish
fillets are cooked and the breadcrumb coating is crunchy and
golden.

Roast trout with almond stuffing

Serves 4

423 calories per serving

Takes 20 minutes to prepare, 20 minutes to cook

calorie controlled cooking spray

1 onion, diced

150 g (5½ oz) mushrooms, chopped finely

110 g (4 oz) ground almonds

15 g (½ oz) anchovies, drained, rinsed and chopped

2 tablespoons capers in brine, rinsed and chopped

finely grated zest and juice of a lime, plus wedges

8 x 90 g (3¼ oz) trout fillets, skin left on

salt and freshly ground black pepper

Two fillets of trout sandwiched together with an almond stuffing and then baked in the oven make a great supper party dish. Serve with steamed green beans and 60 g (2 o. dried brown rice per person, cooked according to the packet instructions.

1 Preheat the oven to Gas Mark 6/200°C/fan oven 180°C. Spray a non stick frying pan with the cooking spray and heat until hot. Add the onion and mushrooms and cook for 5–7 minutes until soft. Remove from the heat and stir in the ground almonds, anchovies, capers and lime zest.

2 Season the fillets on both sides. Line a shallow roasting tin with foil and spray with the cooking spray. Place four fillets skin side down in the tin. Divide the stuffing between the fillets, spread out evenly and squeeze over the lime juice. Top with the other fillets and, to secure, tie together with string in at least tw places. Bake for 20 minutes and serve with the lime wedges.

Provençale trout parcels

Serves 2
174 calories per serving
Takes 15 minutes to prepare,
  20–25 minutes to cook

2 shallots, chopped finely

2 x 250 g (9 oz) whole trout,
  heads left on

4 tomatoes, skinned,
  de-seeded and chopped

4 garlic cloves, crushed

¼ teaspoon fennel seeds,
  crushed

a few fresh thyme sprigs,
  woody stems removed

a few fresh rosemary sprigs,
  woody stems removed

salt and freshly ground black
  pepper

a small bunch of fresh parsley,
  chopped, to garnish

This is a recipe from the South of France. It uses a lot of garlic that mellows in flavour as it bakes.

1 Preheat the oven to Gas Mark 4/180°C/fan oven 160°C and prepare two large squares of non stick baking parchment big enough to parcel up the fish.

2 Place the shallots in the cavities of the fish and then place each fish on a square of paper. Sprinkle over all the other ingredients, except the parsley, and fold up the paper to enclose the fish completely, so that no steam can escape.

3 Place the wrapped fish on a baking tray and bake for 20–25 minutes until cooked through. Serve with the parsley in a small bowl on the table.

Tip... To skin tomatoes, bring a pan of water to the boil. Remove from the heat and then dip the tomatoes into the hot water for a minute. Drain the tomatoes and plunge int cold water. You should now be able to slip off the skins with your hands.

Citrus-crusted salmon

Serves 8

217 calories per serving

Takes 8 minutes to prepare,
15 minutes to cook

750 g (1 lb 10 oz) salmon fillet

4 medium slices white bread,
torn

4 tablespoons chopped fresh
coriander

25 g (1 oz) low fat spread,
melted

grated zest and juice of a
lemon

grated zest and juice of an
orange

salt and freshly ground black
pepper

A whole side of salmon makes for an impressive-looking dish on a buffet, and with a delectable crisp crumb crust, this is positively mouth watering. The salmon can easily be prepared ahead, covered and stored in the fridge until ready to cook.

1 Preheat the oven to Gas Mark 5/190°C/fan oven 170°C. Season the salmon and place on a foil-lined baking tray.

2 Whizz the bread and coriander to fine crumbs in a food processor and then mix with the melted low fat spread, citrus zests and 4 tablespoons of the combined citrus juice. Drizzle the remaining juice over the salmon.

3 Press the crumb crust on to the salmon fillet and then bake in the oven for 15 minutes or until the crust is golden and crisp and the salmon is cooked through. Transfer to a serving platter and serve hot.

Index

Other titles in the Weight Watchers Mini Series

ISBN 978-0-85720-932-0

ISBN 978-0-85720-935-1

ISBN 978-0-85720-934-4

ISBN 978-0-85720-938

ISBN 978-0-85720-931-3

ISBN 978-0-85720-937-5

ISBN 978-0-85720-936-8

ISBN 978-0-85720-933

ISBN 978-1-47111-084-9

ISBN 978-1-47111-089-4

ISBN 978-1-47111-091-7

ISBN 978-1-47111-087

ISBN 978-1-47111-090-0

ISBN 978-1-47111-085-6

ISBN 978-1-47111-088-7

ISBN 978-1-47111-086

For more details please visit www.simonandschuster.co.uk